LIFE AND HEALTH INSURANCE LICENSE EXAM PREP

The Masterclass with Clear-Cut Strategies, State-Specific Questions, and Detailed Explanations to Ensure First-Attempt Success

BLUEPRINT INSTITUTE

SUMMARY (BONUS AT THE END OF THE BOOK)

About the Author

Blueprint Institute is a pioneering company in professional study guides and test preparation, uniquely blending cutting-edge learning technologies with dynamic educational strategies. Established by a collective of certified teachers, digital learning experts and authors, our focus is crafting top-tier educational resources catering to learners across various age groups. Our mission is simple yet profound: transforming learning into an engaging, efficient, and universally accessible journey.

We are dedicated to empowering students with the knowledge and tools they need for academic success. Our approach combines the latest digital learning technology with proven educational methods, ensuring every learner can access top-quality resources.

Our name stands as a commitment to educational excellence and advancement. We are dedicated to ongoing research and developing novel teaching strategies, ensuring every learner can achieve their highest potential.

Join us in navigating a personalized educational path that paves the way to future success!

INTRODUCTION

Welcome to "Life and Health Insurance License Exam Prep - The Masterclass." This guide will help you prepare for the life and health insurance licensing exam. It's not just a manual but a comprehensive course designed to ensure your success on the first attempt. We provide you with all the tools necessary to approach the exam with confidence and expertise, including targeted strategies, state-specific questions, and innovative flashcards. The insurance industry requires a deep and thorough understanding of numerous theoretical concepts, regulatory laws, and operational procedures. Our goal is to arm you with a complete and detailed knowledge of these elements so that you can pass the exam and embark on a successful career in the insurance sector.

The book is structured into three main sections. The first section is the core of your theoretical preparation. It comprises five chapters discussing fifty fundamental topics across every life and health insurance facet. From "The Role of Insurance" and "Key Terminology" to "Policies and Claims Processes," each chapter is organized to facilitate progressive and integrated learning.

We begin with an overview of insurance basics, exploring fundamental principles and types of coverage. As you progress, the focus shifts to the specifics of life and health insurance, examining different insurance products and their applications. We also cover regulatory aspects critical for operating within the law. The final chapter on exam preparation offers effective study techniques, time management advice, and strategies for dealing with exam day jitters. Following the theoretical foundation, you'll move to the second section, which features seventy multiple-choice questions that simulate the natural exam environment. This allows you to test your knowledge in practical scenarios, with each question crafted to reflect the standards of licensing exams and provide an experience as close to the real thing as possible.

The third and final section of the book is dedicated to answers and detailed explanations for the questions posed in the previous section. Each answer is accompanied by a thorough explanation that confirms the correctness of the response and helps you understand the rationale behind it. This approach is critical for exam preparation, as it reinforces concept comprehension and addresses gaps in understanding. To maximize the benefits of "Life and Health Insurance License Exam Prep - The Masterclass," we recommend following the sections in order. Begin with the theory to build a solid foundation of knowledge, then test what you've learned with the multiple-choice questions, and finally, review the explanations to clear any doubts and strengthen your understanding.

This book is designed to support you at every stage of your preparation, providing tools to confidently approach the exam and emerge as a qualified professional in the insurance field. We hope the journey you've chosen to embark on with our book is informative and inspiring.

Good luck with your studies, and best wishes for your exam!

CHAPTER 1

UNDERSTANDING THE FUNDAMENTALS

In this chapter, we initiate your journey into the insurance world by dissecting "The Role of Insurance." This crucial starting point demystifies how insurance functions as a cornerstone of personal financial security and economic stability. Insurance, at its core, is a risk-transfer mechanism. Individuals and entities purchase insurance to transfer the financial risks of life's uncertainties to an insurer. In exchange for premium payments, the insurer promises to cover financial losses related to specified events or mishaps, such as illness, property damage, or the death of a wage earner.

The importance of insurance extends beyond individual benefits. It plays a pivotal role in the broader economy by providing the security necessary for people to invest in their businesses, purchase homes, and save for the future without the paralyzing fear of total loss. By pooling the risks of many individuals and organizations, insurance companies can distribute the financial impact of losses across a wider community, thereby mitigating the adverse effects of significant economic burdens on any single entity.

Moreover, insurance drives a substantial part of the financial services sector, involving a complex interplay of actuarial science, risk assessment, and claims management. This sector protects assets and generates vast amounts of capital through its operations. Insurers invest premiums into various financial instruments, such as bonds, stocks, and real estate, contributing significantly to capital markets' liquidity and stability.

This chapter lays the groundwork for understanding how essential insurance is in managing personal risks, facilitating commercial activities, and fostering a stable environment conducive to economic growth. Through this exploration, you will understand why insurance is not merely a financial safety net but also a fundamental enabler of modern economies. This foundational knowledge sets the stage for deeper insights into specific types of insurance, principles, and processes covered in subsequent chapter sections.

THE ROLE OF INSURANCE

The role of insurance is crucial for both individuals and the broader economy. It is an essential economic tool to manage daily risks, a concept known as risk transfer. Policyholders can transfer the cost of potential loss to an insurance company, which agrees to cover losses in exchange for premium payments.

Insurance helps to mitigate the uncertainty of life's various risks. These risks range from routine car accidents and home damage to significant health crises and business interruptions. Individuals and businesses must set aside substantial financial reserves to cover these potential losses without insurance. This would immobilize a significant portion of capital, limiting the ability to invest in growth opportunities. Insurance liberates these resources, allowing for personal and economic development by providing a safety net that reduces the need for excessive precautionary savings. At its core, the insurance industry underpins economic activity by fostering a more predictable environment where people are more likely to undertake investments and engage in activities that could be prohibitively risky without coverage. For example, entrepreneurs are more inclined to start businesses, homeowners are more likely to purchase houses, and car buyers are more willing to invest in vehicles, knowing that their investments are protected against catastrophic losses.

Furthermore, insurance plays a vital role in promoting financial stability. By pooling the risks of many policyholders, insurance companies can distribute the cost of claims among a broad base, effectively reducing losses' economic impact on any individual. This risk pooling is not just a foundational strategy of insurance but also a principle supporting community and societal stability. Insurance payouts provide critical financial support for recovery efforts in large-scale disasters, such as hurricanes or earthquakes, helping stabilize local economies quickly.

Moreover, the insurance sector is a significant contributor to the financial markets. The premiums collected are invested in various financial instruments, including government securities, corporate bonds, and real estate. These investments are crucial for the liquidity of financial markets and help fund municipal and infrastructure projects that might otherwise lack sufficient funding. Thus, the role of insurance extends far beyond simple coverage for unforeseen events; it is a sophisticated economic instrument that supports public welfare, fosters economic growth, and facilitates the functioning of financial markets. By understanding these dynamics, individuals and businesses can appreciate the protective aspects of insurance and its broader contributions to economic and social stability.

KEY TERMINOLOGY

1. **Actuary** - A professional who analyzes the financial consequences of risk and uncertainty, using mathematics, statistics, and economic theory to assess events' probability and financial impact.

2. **Adjuster** - An insurance professional who evaluates the extent of the insurer's liability in the settlement of a claim.

3. **Agent** - A person who sells and services insurance policies on behalf of an insurance company.

4. **Annuity** - A financial product that pays out a fixed stream of payments to an individual, primarily used as an income stream for retirees.

5. **Application** - A form an insurance company uses to gather information about a prospective policyholder to determine eligibility for coverage.

6. **Beneficiary** - The person or entity designated to receive the benefits from an insurance policy, typically in the context of life insurance.

7. **Binder** - A temporary insurance contract that provides proof of coverage until a permanent policy is issued.

8. **Broker** - An individual who arranges and negotiates insurance coverage by representing the client rather than the insurer.

9. **Captive Agent** - An insurance agent who sells insurance for only one company.

10. **Claim** - A request for payment under the terms of an insurance policy after a loss has occurred.

11. **Coinsurance** - A provision that requires the policyholder to pay a specified percentage of the costs of covered services after the deductible has been paid.

12. **Commission** - The fee paid to an agent or broker for selling an insurer's products.

13. **Coverage** - The scope of protection provided under an insurance policy.

14. **Deductible** - A policyholder must pay out of pocket before the insurance company pays a claim.

15. **Endorsement** - An amendment to an existing insurance policy that changes the terms or scope of coverage.

16. **Exclusion** - Specific conditions or circumstances listed in the policy that are not covered by the insurance policy.

17. **Expiry** - The date on which an insurance policy terminates.

18. **Floater** - A type of insurance coverage that applies to movable or transportable property, offering protection for assets not tied to a specific location.

19. **Grace Period** - After the premium due date, an overdue payment can be made without penalty.

20. **Group Insurance** - Insurance that covers a group of people, typically company employees, under one contract.

21. **Guaranteed Replacement Cost** - Coverage that pays the total cost of replacing damaged property without a depreciation deduction and regardless of the policy's limits.

22. **Indemnity** - A principle that ensures an insurance policy should not provide a benefit greater than the loss suffered by the insured.

23. **Insurable Interest** - A requirement that the policyholder must be at risk of financial loss from a covered event in order to purchase insurance.

24. **Insured** - The person or entity covered by an insurance policy.

25. **Insurer** - The company that issues and underwrites an insurance policy.

26. **Liability Insurance** - Insurance that provides protection against claims alleging that a property owner's negligence or inappropriate action resulted in bodily injury or property damage to another party.

27. **Limit** - The maximum amount an insurance company will pay for a covered loss.

28. **Loss** - The injury or damage sustained by the insured that the insurer agrees to cover under the terms of the policy.

29. **Moral Hazard** - The tendency of a person insured against a risk to behave differently than if they bore the full cost of the risk themselves.

30. **Named Peril** - A hazard that an insurance policy specifically covers.

31. **No-Fault Insurance** - A type of insurance where the insured is reimbursed by their own insurer regardless of fault.

32. **Non-renewal** - A decision by an insurer not to renew a policy at the end of its term.

33. **Peril** - A specific risk or cause of loss covered by an insurance policy, such as fire, windstorm, flood, or theft.

34. **Policy** - The contract issued by an insurance company to the insured that outlines the terms and conditions of the coverage.

35. **Premium** - The payment made by the insured to the insurance company in exchange for insurance coverage.

36. **Provision** - A clause in an insurance policy that stipulates a condition or requirement.

37. **Quote** - An estimate of the premium for the insurance coverage requested by an applicant.

38. **Rate** - The cost of a unit of insurance.

39. **Reinsurance** - The practice whereby insurers transfer portions of risk portfolios to other parties to reduce the likelihood of paying a large obligation resulting from an insurance claim.

40. **Renewal** - The continuation of an insurance policy into a new term.

41. **Rider** - An addition to an insurance policy that alters coverage or terms.

42. **Risk** - The possibility that a loss may occur.

43. **Settlement** - An agreement reached between the insurer and the insured to resolve a claim.

44. **Subrogation** - The process by which an insurance company, having paid off a loss, recovers the amount paid from a third party responsible for causing the loss.

45. **Term** - The period of time for which an insurance policy is in effect.

46. **Third Party** - A person other than the policyholder or insurer who has incurred losses or is entitled to receive payment due to acts or omissions of the policyholder.

47. **Underwriter** - The individual at an insurance company who evaluates and accepts or rejects risks, determining the terms and conditions of coverage.

48. **Underwriting** - The process of evaluating a risk and determining whether to insure it and under what terms.

49. **Unearned Premium** - The portion of a premium that has been collected by the insurer but not yet earned because the policy period has not yet expired.

50. **Waiver** - An agreement in an insurance contract that allows a party to relinquish a known right, claim, or privilege.

TYPES OF LIFE INSURANCE

In Chapter 1 of "Understanding the Fundamentals," we explore various types of life insurance available, providing a comprehensive overview of each to ensure policyholders can make informed decisions that suit their financial and personal circumstances. Life insurance is a critical component in financial planning, offering peace of mind that beneficiaries will be supported financially upon the policyholder's death. Here, we delve into the primary types of life insurance policies:

1. **Term Life Insurance**: This is the simplest and most accessible form of life insurance, offering coverage for a specified period or "term"—usually 10, 20, or 30 years. The beneficiaries receive the death benefit if the policyholder dies within this term. Term life insurance is often favored for its lower initial premiums compared to permanent life insurance, making it an attractive option for individuals seeking significant coverage on

a limited budget. However, it does not build cash value. Once the term expires, the policyholder must seek new coverage, often at higher rates due to increased age or changes in health.

2. **Whole Life Insurance**: Unlike term insurance, whole life insurance provides lifelong coverage as long as premiums are paid. This type of policy also includes an investment component known as the cash value, which grows at a guaranteed rate over time. Policyholders can borrow against the cash value or surrender the policy for the cash value, although this may reduce the death benefit. Whole life insurance premiums are higher than term life premiums due to the accumulation of lifetime coverage and cash value.

3. **Universal Life Insurance**: This flexible policy allows the policyholder to adjust the premiums and death benefits. Universal life insurance also features a savings element that grows on a tax-deferred basis. The interest rate applied to the cash value component may vary, but some policies offer a minimum guaranteed rate. The flexibility of universal life insurance is a significant advantage, but it requires active management to ensure that the cash value is sufficient to sustain the policy, especially if premiums are adjusted frequently.

4. **Variable Life Insurance**: With variable life insurance, the policyholder can invest the cash value in various separate accounts, ranging from stocks and bonds to money market funds. This type of insurance is suitable for those who are willing to take on investment risks for the possibility of greater returns. The cash value and death benefit can fluctuate based on the performance of the invested assets, although some policies may offer a guaranteed minimum death benefit.

5. **Variable Universal Life Insurance**: Combining the features of variable and universal life insurance, this policy offers both the investment options of variable life insurance and the flexibility of universal life insurance. Policyholders can adjust premiums and death benefits and choose how to invest the cash value. This type of insurance is complex and best suited for those who understand investment strategies and are comfortable with assuming risk.

Each of these life insurance types serves different financial needs and risk tolerances. Term life insurance is often recommended for those with a temporary need for coverage or a limited budget. In contrast, whole, universal, and variable policies are better suited for long-term financial planning, offering death benefits and wealth accumulation opportunities. Understanding these options allows individuals to choose a policy that best matches their long-term financial goals and provides their beneficiaries with the desired level of security.

TYPES OF HEALTH INSURANCE

Health insurance is essential for providing financial protection in case of medical expenses. It is a type of insurance coverage that pays for medical and surgical expenses incurred by the insured. Health insurance can either reimburse the insured for expenses incurred from illness or injury or pay the care provider directly.

Major Types of Health Insurance

1. **Individual Private Health Insurance**

   - **Description**: This is coverage that individuals purchase for themselves or for their families. Individual plans can be customized to fit the insured's specific health needs and budget.

   - **Benefits**: Offers flexibility in the choice of coverage and providers.

   - **Limitations**: Typically more expensive than group insurance and may offer less comprehensive coverage.

2. **Group Health Insurance**

   - **Description**: Also known as employer-sponsored health insurance, this is typically provided by an employer and offers the same benefits to all participating employees.

   - **Benefits**: Often subsidized by the employer, making it less expensive for employees.

   - **Limitations**: Limited choice in terms of plan options and providers.

3. **Managed Care Plans**

   - These plans contract with health care providers and medical facilities to provide care for members at reduced costs. These include:

     - **Health Maintenance Organizations (HMOs)**: Require members to obtain care from a network of designated providers and to choose a primary care physician to oversee all treatment.

     - **Preferred Provider Organizations (PPOs)**: Offer more flexibility in selecting a provider and do not always require a primary care physician's referral.

     - **Exclusive Provider Organizations (EPOs)**: A hybrid of HMO and PPO, these plans require you to use a network of providers, but do not usually require referrals for specialists.

   - **Benefits**: Lower costs due to negotiated rates.

   - **Limitations**: Less freedom to choose providers outside of the network.

4. **High-Deductible Health Plan (HDHP)**

   - **Description**: Features higher deductibles than traditional insurance plans. Can be combined with a Health Savings Account (HSA), allowing individuals to save money tax-free against medical expenses.

   - **Benefits**: Lower premiums and tax benefits.

   - **Limitations**: Higher out-of-pocket costs until the deductible is met.

5. **Medicare**

   - **Description**: A federal program providing health coverage if you are 65+ or under 65 and with a disability, no matter your income.

   - **Parts**:

     - **Part A (Hospital Insurance)**: Covers inpatient hospital stays, care in a skilled nursing facility, hospice care, and some home health care.

     - **Part B (Medical Insurance)**: Covers certain doctors' services, outpatient care, medical supplies, and preventive services.

     - **Part C (Medicare Advantage Plans)**: Offers all benefits and services covered under Part A and Part B, usually includes Medicare prescription drug coverage (Part D) as part of the plan.

     - **Part D (prescription drug coverage)**: Adds prescription drug coverage to Original Medicare, some Medicare Cost Plans, some Medicare Private-Fee-for-Service Plans, and Medicare Medical Savings Account Plans.

   - **Benefits**: Broad coverage, especially for seniors.

   - **Limitations**: Parts A and B have limited prescription drug coverage, necessitating additional Part D coverage.

6. **Medicaid**

   - **Description**: A state and federal program that provides health coverage if you have a very low income.

   - **Benefits**: Comprehensive coverage with minimal co-pays.

   - **Limitations**: Eligibility depends on state-specific criteria.

7. **Catastrophic Health Insurance**

   - **Description**: Provides coverage for medical emergencies, protecting against massive medical costs that can occur due to serious illness or injury.

- **Benefits**: Lower premiums.
- **Limitations**: High deductibles, generally only available to people under 30 or those with hardship exemptions.

8. **Supplemental Health Insurance**

- **Description**: Additional coverage that can be purchased to handle expenses that your regular insurance does not cover, such as cancer policies.
- **Benefits**: Covers additional expenses like travel costs, lost income, childcare, and home care.
- **Limitations**: Does not replace comprehensive health coverage and adds an additional cost.

INSURANCE PRINCIPLES

These principles are crucial for understanding how insurance policies are structured, priced, and how risk is managed. They ensure the functionality and viability of insurance as a financial tool and maintain equity and fairness for both the insurer and the insured.

Principle of Utmost Good Faith (Uberrima Fides)

At the heart of insurance transactions is the principle of utmost good faith, which requires both the insurer and the insured to act honestly and not mislead or withhold critical information from one another. This principle is foundational because insurance is a contract based on trust. The insured must provide accurate and complete information regarding their health, financial status, or any other factor that may influence the insurer's decision to cover the risk. Similarly, the insurer must clearly and honestly disclose the insurance policy's terms, benefits, and limitations.

Principle of Insurable Interest

For an insurance contract to be valid, the policyholder must demonstrate an insurable interest in the risk being covered. This means the policyholder would suffer a financial loss or certain other kinds of losses if the insured event occurs. For instance, individuals have an insurable interest in their own lives and the lives of their family members or business partners. Without insurable interest, the insurance contract could be considered an illegal gambling contract. This principle prevents moral hazard and reduces the potential for insurance fraud.

Principle of Indemnity

This principle ensures that insurance policies provide a benefit no greater than the loss suffered by the insured. The purpose of insurance is not to allow the insured to profit from their loss but to restore them to approximately the same financial position they were in before the loss occurred. Indemnity is fundamental to property and casualty insurance. Still, it does not typically apply to life insurance, where a specified sum is agreed upon in advance.

Principle of Contribution

Contribution is a corollary to the principle of indemnity and applies when multiple insurance policies insure the same risk. It prevents the insured from claiming the full amount of loss from multiple insurers. Instead, each insurer contributes proportionally to the loss up to the limit of their respective policies. This principle ensures that the claim does not exceed the actual value of the loss and helps maintain the principle of indemnity across multiple policies.

Principle of Subrogation

After compensating the insured for a loss, an insurer may invoke the principle of subrogation to assume the insured's legal right to pursue a third party responsible for the loss. This allows the insurer to seek recovery of the amount paid to the insured from the third party. Subrogation mitigates the cost of claims and discourages negligence and misconduct by third parties. It also ensures that insurers can reclaim some of the costs they incur in claims, which can help keep insurance premiums more affordable for all policyholders.

Principle of Proximate Cause

The principle of proximate cause is used to determine whether a loss results from an insured peril. In an unbroken sequence, it identifies which peril or event is the closest to the loss. This principle is fundamental in complex scenarios where multiple events contribute to the loss. Understanding proximate cause helps insurers and insureds determine if the policy covers the loss and which peril to attribute it to.

Each of these principles plays a critical role in the functioning of insurance policies and the industry at large. They ensure that while insurers provide the financial security promised, policyholders uphold their part of the agreement, maintaining a balance that allows the insurance industry to operate effectively and reliably.

UNDERSTANDING RISK MANAGEMENT

In the continuum of "Understanding the Fundamentals" within our guidebook, "Life and Health Insurance License Exam Prep - The Masterclass," we move from the underlying principles of insurance to the essential concept of risk management. Risk management is a systematic process crucial for individuals and organizations, particularly within the insurance sector. It involves identifying, assessing, and prioritizing risks followed by coordinated and economical application of resources to minimize, monitor, and control the probability or impact of unfortunate events or maximize opportunities' realization.

Understanding Risk Management

Risk management in insurance is not just about identifying potential risks; it's about understanding and mitigating them effectively. It entails a deep dive into the potential risks a policyholder might face and the risks the insurer accepts when underwriting new policies. For insurers, effective risk management means balancing the risks they insure and the premiums they charge to ensure profitability and financial stability.

Steps in the Risk Management Process

1. **Risk Identification**: This is the first and perhaps the most critical step in the risk management process. It involves the systematic recognition of potential risks that could negatively impact an individual's health, property, or life. This could be as simple as identifying the risk of theft for a property insurance policy or as complex as recognizing the various risks associated with providing health insurance in different regions.

2. **Risk Assessment**: Once risks are identified, they must be assessed regarding their potential severity and the likelihood of occurrence. This assessment helps prioritize which risks need more immediate attention or robust safeguards. For instance, a health insurance provider may prioritize covering chronic diseases like diabetes more than temporary conditions based on prevalence data.

3. **Risk Control**: After assessing the risks, steps must be taken to control or mitigate them. This can involve avoiding the risk altogether, reducing the negative effect of the risk, or accepting some or all of the consequences of a particular risk. For example, an insurer may decide not to cover homes in a flood-prone area (risk avoidance) or may offer coverage with a higher deductible (risk reduction).

4. **Risk Financing**: This involves deciding how to fund the risks that have been accepted. It includes strategies like retaining the risk (self-insurance), transferring the risk to another party (buying insurance), or sharing the risk (through co-insurance arrangements).

Risk Management Techniques in Insurance

In practice, insurance companies employ various techniques to manage risks:

- **Underwriting Standards**: Insurers implement strict underwriting criteria to ensure they do not take on policyholders whose risk level exceeds acceptable thresholds. These standards help in assessing the risk associated with an application effectively.

- **Diversification**: By underwriting a diverse range of insurance policies, insurers spread their risk across different policyholders, geographic regions, and types of insurance. This helps in mitigating the impact of a loss in one area.

- **Reinsurance**: Insurers transfer portions of their risk portfolios to other parties by buying reinsurance. This helps them recover from significant losses that may occur due to catastrophic events or large claims.

- **Claims Management**: Efficient claims management can significantly reduce the insurer's risk. This involves timely and fair handling of claims and implementing measures to combat fraud and reduce the incidence of inflated claims.

Effective risk management is fundamental in insurance and plays a pivotal role in the stability and profitability of insurers. It also ensures policyholders receive the protection they expect without undue delay or hassle. This meticulous approach to risk not only aids insurers in maintaining a healthy portfolio but also instills confidence among policyholders, thereby enhancing the overall trust and reliability perceived by the insurer.

THE UNDERWRITING PROCESS

The underwriting process in insurance is a critical procedure where insurers evaluate and analyze the risks associated with insuring a potential policyholder. This process is fundamental to the industry because it determines which risks are acceptable to insure, under what conditions, and at what price. Underwriting ensures that the premium the insured pays is commensurate with the risk the insurer accepts.

Overview of the Underwriting Process

Underwriting in insurance is both an art and a science, involving a blend of statistical analysis and human judgment. The goal is to protect the insurance company's solvency while offering fair terms and rates to customers. The process can vary significantly between different types of insurance, such as health, life, auto, or property insurance, but the core steps generally include:

1. **Information Gathering**: The first step in the underwriting process is gathering pertinent information about the applicant. This can include personal information, medical histories, lifestyle, the condition of property, driving records, or any other relevant data. Life and health insurance might involve a medical examination or a detailed health questionnaire. Auto insurance might include checking the driving history.

2. **Risk Evaluation**: Once sufficient information is gathered, the underwriter evaluates the risk associated with insuring the applicant. This involves analyzing the collected data to estimate a claim's likelihood and potential severity. Actuarial data, historical claims statistics, and risk prediction models are often used to assist in this evaluation.

3. **Rating and Pricing**: Based on the risk evaluation, the underwriter assigns a rating to the applicant that determines the premium they will be charged. Applicants considered lower risk will be offered lower premiums, whereas higher risk individuals might face higher premiums or even denial of coverage. The rating process is crucial as it ensures that the premium is proportional to the risk, maintaining the insurer's profitability and ability to cover all claims.

4. **Policy Issuance**: If the applicant accepts the offered terms and premium, the policy is issued. The underwriter prepares the insurance policy that outlines the terms of coverage, limits, premiums, and other conditions. This policy is a legal contract binding both the insurer and the insured.

Challenges in Underwriting

Underwriting involves significant challenges, such as accurately assessing risk in complex scenarios or dealing with incomplete information. Advancements in data analytics, machine learning, and artificial intelligence are increasingly being used to enhance the precision of risk assessment models and streamline the information-gathering and evaluation phases.

Ethical and Regulatory Considerations

Underwriters must navigate ethical and regulatory landscapes. They must ensure fair treatment of applicants and avoid practices such as unjust discrimination. Regulations may dictate certain underwriting practices, especially in health insurance, where factors like pre-existing conditions can no longer be used to deny coverage in many jurisdictions.

The Role of Technology in Underwriting

Technological advancements have profoundly transformed the underwriting process. Automated underwriting systems allow for quicker decision-making by rapidly processing large data sets. These systems can provide immediate risk assessments and policy pricing, significantly speeding up the process for standard applications. However, human underwriters remain essential in interpreting nuanced information and making informed judgments for more complex cases.

The underwriting process is indispensable in insurance, balancing the needs of policyholders for fair and affordable coverage with the necessity for insurers to manage risk effectively. As the insurance landscape evolves with changes in technology, regulation, and market conditions, underwriting will continue to adapt, ensuring the industry's resilience and relevance. This meticulous approach to assessing and pricing risk sustains insurance companies' viability. It provides security for the countless individuals and entities that rely on insurance protection daily.

BENEFICIARIES

In the insurance world, understanding the role and importance of beneficiaries is essential for anyone entering into an insurance contract. Beneficiaries are the individuals or entities designated by the policyholder to receive the benefits or payout from an insurance policy, typically in the event of the policyholder's death. This section of Chapter 1, "Understanding the Fundamentals," delves into the intricacies of designating beneficiaries, the types of beneficiaries, and the legal considerations involved.

A beneficiary can be a person, a group of people, a trust, or even an organization, such as a charity. In the context of life insurance, beneficiaries are primarily those who will receive the policy's death benefits. For other types of insurance, like health or property, the beneficiary might be the insured themselves or a dependent who benefits from the policy's coverage.

Types of Beneficiaries

1. **Primary Beneficiaries**: These are the first in line to receive the death benefits of an insurance policy. Policyholders can name one or multiple primary beneficiaries and specify the percentage of the payout each one will receive.

2. **Contingent or Secondary Beneficiaries**: Contingent beneficiaries are next in line if the primary beneficiary is deceased or unable to accept the benefits. Their inclusion ensures that the benefits will be distributed according to the policyholder's wishes, even if the primary beneficiaries cannot claim them.

3. **Revocable and Irrevocable Beneficiaries**: Policyholders can designate beneficiaries as revocable, which allows them to change beneficiaries without the consent of the current beneficiaries. In contrast, irrevocable beneficiaries cannot be changed without the beneficiary's consent. This designation is often used to ensure that the beneficiary's interest in the policy is protected and cannot be easily altered.

Legal Considerations

When naming beneficiaries, several legal considerations must be taken into account to ensure the process is handled correctly:

- **Clarity and Specificity**: It's critical to clearly identify each beneficiary by using full names and, where possible, other identifying information to prevent any disputes or confusion about the policyholder's intentions after their death.

- **Minor Beneficiaries**: If the beneficiary is a minor, the policyholder must arrange for a legal guardian or establish a trust to manage the proceeds until the child reaches legal age. Failure to do so can complicate the process and potentially delay the distribution of benefits.

- **Updates and Changes**: Life changes such as marriage, divorce, the birth of a child, or the death of a designated beneficiary should prompt a review and, if necessary, an update to the beneficiary designations. This ensures that the benefits will go to the appropriate individuals as intended.

The Role of Beneficiaries in Estate Planning

Beneficiaries are a critical component of estate planning. Designating beneficiaries for insurance policies can be a strategic way to distribute assets to loved ones or organizations while potentially bypassing the lengthy and public process of probate. This makes understanding and carefully choosing beneficiaries an essential part of financial and estate planning. The selection of beneficiaries is a significant decision that requires careful consideration and, often, legal guidance. By designating beneficiaries, a policyholder can ensure that their insurance benefits are passed on according to their wishes, providing financial support or a legacy to those they care about most. This function of beneficiaries underscores the personal and financial importance of insurance policies, beyond mere risk mitigation, extending into thoughtful estate management and planning.

PREMIUMS AND POLICIES

Premiums are the payments made by the policyholder to the insurance company in exchange for the coverage detailed in the policy. These payments can be scheduled at various intervals—annually, semi-annually, quarterly, or monthly, depending on the terms agreed upon. The amount of the premium is influenced by several factors including, but not limited to, the type of coverage, the insured's risk profile, the policy limits, and the length of coverage.

1. **Risk Assessment**: One of the primary determinants of premium cost is the level of risk the insurer takes on. This is assessed during the underwriting process where factors such as age, health, lifestyle, and property insurance, location and property value are considered. Higher risks typically attract higher premiums.

2. **Type of Insurance**: Different types of insurance policies have different premium structures. Life insurance premiums, for example, may vary significantly from health insurance premiums due to the differing nature of risk and coverage.

3. **Policy Limits and Deductibles**: The amount of coverage and the deductible chosen also impact premium amounts. Higher coverage limits and lower deductibles usually result in higher premiums because the insurer is required to pay out more in the event of a claim.

Components of Insurance Policies

An insurance policy is a legal document that outlines the terms and conditions of the insurance contract. It specifies what risks are covered, the limits of coverage, the premium amount, and the policy duration, among other crucial details. Understanding the following key components is vital for effectively managing and utilizing insurance:

1. **Declarations Page**: Often the first part of an insurance policy, the declarations page summarizes key information including the insured's name, the policy effective dates, coverage amounts, and the premium.

2. **Insuring Agreement**: This section details the obligations of the insurance company and what risks are covered under the policy. It essentially lays out the promise of the insurer to pay for certain losses attributed to specific perils.

3. **Exclusions**: Exclusions are critical in defining what is not covered by the policy. These clauses restrict the scope of the policy and direct the insured on scenarios and events that will not lead to a payout.

4. **Conditions**: These are the rules set by the insurance policy for both the insurer and the insured. Conditions might include the requirement to pay premiums on time, the process for filing a claim, and the steps to follow if there is a disagreement about the policy's coverage or terms.

5. **Endorsements**: Also known as riders, endorsements modify the original policy terms by adding or subtracting coverage. They are used to customize a policy to fit specific needs beyond standard offerings.

The Importance of Regular Policy Review

Regularly reviewing one's insurance policy is essential. Life events such as marriage, the birth of a child, a new job, or significant changes in health can affect coverage needs. Additionally, market conditions and law changes might influence the appropriate and cost-effective coverage.

Premiums and policies are fundamental insurance aspects that dictate the coverage dynamics and financial relationship between the insured and the insurer. Understanding these elements allows policyholders to make informed decisions about their insurance needs and manage their policies effectively to ensure optimal coverage and financial stability. As such, mastery of this information is advantageous and essential for anyone looking to navigate the complexities of insurance.

CLAIMS PROCESS

The claims process is a critical component of the insurance framework, serving as the practical application of the policy when it is most needed: when a loss occurs.

Overview of the Claims Process

The claims process is when an insured person requests payment from an insurance company for a covered loss. This process begins when a claim is filed and ends when the claim is settled, or the insurer compensates the insured or a third-party claimant. Effective management of this process is essential for maintaining customer satisfaction and trust in the insurance provider.

Steps in the Claims Process

1. **Notification of the Claim**: The first step in the claims process is the notification of a loss. Policyholders must inform their insurance company as soon as possible after an incident occurs. This notification should include all pertinent details of the loss, including the date, location, and extent of damage.

2. **Claim Filing**: The insured must fill out a claim form, providing a formal description of the event and the damages incurred. This form serves as the official request for compensation. Accuracy and completeness of information here are crucial to ensure a smooth process.

3. **Claim Investigation**: Once a claim is filed, the insurance company reviews and investigates it to verify the details and determine its validity. This investigation may involve assessing physical damage, interviewing witnesses, or reviewing relevant documents such as police reports or medical records.

4. **Adjustment and Evaluation**: An insurance adjuster is typically assigned to the claim to evaluate the loss and determine the amount of payment. The adjuster's role is to inspect the damage, assess what repairs are needed, and calculate the cost of these repairs. This stage may also involve negotiation between the adjuster and the policyholder to reach an agreement on the compensation amount.

5. **Resolution and Payment**: After the claim evaluation is completed and any necessary negotiations are concluded, the insurer will issue payment to the insured or an approved third-party. The amount paid is based on the policy terms and the evaluation conducted by the adjuster.

6. **Closure of the Claim**: Once the payment is made, the claim is considered resolved, and the case is closed, unless there are subsequent disputes about the claim.

Challenges in the Claims Process

The claims process can be fraught with challenges that require careful navigation. Delays can occur due to incomplete documentation, lack of necessary approvals, or disputes over the cause of damage or the coverage. Furthermore, if a claim is denied, policyholders may need to engage in a dispute resolution process, which can prolong the situation.

Transparency during the claims process is vital for maintaining trust between the insurer and the insured. Clear communication about each step, expected timelines, and any arising issues or delays is crucial. Insurers that manage this process effectively are more likely to retain their customers and uphold their reputation in the industry.

CHAPTER 2

LIFE INSURANCE IN DETAIL

TERM LIFE INSURANCE

Term life insurance is a fundamental type of life insurance policy designed to provide financial protection over a specific period, known as the "term." This policy is straightforward and economical, making it a preferred choice for individuals seeking short-term, high-value coverage.

Definition and Structure

Term life insurance policies provide coverage for a predetermined period, typically ranging from 5 to 30 years. If the insured person passes away during this term, the policy pays out a death benefit to the named beneficiaries. This type of insurance is characterized by fixed premiums and a fixed death benefit, which do not change throughout the term. Term life insurance does not accumulate cash value, which distinguishes it from permanent life insurance options.

Advantages of Term Life Insurance

One of the primary advantages of term life insurance is its affordability. Because these policies do not include an investment component and only offer coverage for a limited time, the premiums are considerably lower than those for permanent life insurance. This cost-effectiveness makes term life insurance accessible, allowing policyholders to obtain higher levels of coverage at a lower cost, which is particularly valuable during peak years of financial obligation.

Another significant benefit is the simplicity of the product. Term life insurance policies are easy to understand, making them an excellent choice for individuals who are new to life insurance. The straightforward nature of term life insurance also simplifies the decision-making process for buyers, as they can focus primarily on the term length and coverage amount without needing to understand more complex features like cash value or investment options.

Flexibility and Conversion

Many term life insurance policies include a conversion feature, allowing the policyholder to convert their term policy into a permanent one without undergoing further medical underwriting. This option is invaluable for those who may develop health issues during the term and face challenges in obtaining new life insurance coverage. Converting a term policy to a permanent one ensures that coverage continues irrespective of health changes, albeit with an increase in premiums reflective of the permanent policy's benefits.

Ideal Use Cases

Term life insurance is ideally suited for individuals and families with specific, time-bound financial responsibilities. For example, parents with young children might choose a term that covers the years through college graduation, ensuring financial support for their children in the event of an untimely death. Similarly, homeowners might align the term with the duration of their mortgage payments, providing security against the possibility of leaving behind financial burdens.

Limitations

The primary limitation of term life insurance is that coverage is temporary and can potentially expire before the policyholder dies. Suppose the term ends and the insured is still living. In that case, the coverage ceases without any benefit payout, and there is no accumulated cash value to recover. While this is often acceptable given the lower cost, it does require policyholders to potentially face higher premiums or difficulties in obtaining new coverage at an older age or with changed health conditions.

Term life insurance is an essential risk management tool, offering substantial protection during periods of high financial exposure at an affordable cost. It is tailored for those needing coverage to match specific financial obligations' timing, providing peace of mind with minimal financial outlay. Understanding the specific attributes and suitability of term life insurance can guide individuals in making informed decisions about their life insurance needs.

WHOLE LIFE INSURANCE

Whole life insurance is a type of permanent life insurance that offers lifelong coverage alongside an investment component known as cash value, which grows over time. As one of the most comprehensive forms of life insurance available, whole life insurance provides a death benefit and a financial asset that accumulates value, making it a cornerstone of long-term financial planning.

Unlike term life insurance, which provides coverage for a specific period, whole life insurance remains in effect for the insured's entire life, provided premiums are paid. This enduring coverage is complemented by fixed premium rates that do not increase with age or changes in health, offering predictable costs that can be essential for long-term budgeting. The stability of premium costs, despite potentially rising health care costs and inflation, is a significant advantage, ensuring that coverage remains affordable throughout the insured's life.

One of the distinguishing features of whole life insurance is the cash value component. Part of each premium payment is allocated to this cash value, which grows at a guaranteed rate set by the insurance company. Over time, this cash value accumulates on a tax-deferred basis, which means taxes on gains are deferred until the money is withdrawn. Policyholders can tap into this cash value through loans or direct withdrawals, providing a source of funds for opportunities or emergencies. However, managing these withdrawals carefully is important as they can reduce the policy's death benefit and overall value.

The cash value also provides financial flexibility. For instance, if financial circumstances change, policyholders can sometimes use the accumulated cash value to cover premium payments, keeping the policy active even during challenging financial times. Additionally, if the cash value grows sufficiently, it can eventually reach a point where it fully covers the ongoing premium payments, making the policy "paid up." This means that the insured enjoys coverage without further out-of-pocket expenses.

Another significant benefit of whole life insurance is its role in estate planning. The death benefit provided by whole-life policies is generally tax-free. It is paid directly to beneficiaries upon the policyholder's death, providing a straightforward way to transfer wealth without the complexities and delays of probate. This feature makes whole life insurance an attractive option for those looking to secure a financial legacy for their heirs. Moreover, whole life insurance offers potential dividends depending on the insurer's financial performance. While not guaranteed, these dividends can be used to purchase additional coverage, reduce future premiums, or even be received in cash, providing further financial benefits to policyholders.

Whole life insurance is more than just an insurance product; it is a versatile financial tool that provides security and peace of mind. With its guaranteed death benefit, fixed premiums, and a cash value for multiple financial purposes, whole life insurance remains a popular choice for individuals looking to combine risk management with investment growth. Whole life insurance offers a robust and attractive solution for those committed to long-term financial planning and seeking a reliable means to protect and enhance their financial legacy.

UNIVERSAL LIFE INSURANCE

Universal life insurance is a type of permanent life insurance that combines flexibility in premiums and coverage with the ability to accumulate cash value, making it a sophisticated financial planning tool well suited to those seeking customizable life insurance solutions. This type of life insurance is characterized by adjustable premiums and the ability to adjust the death benefit, giving policyholders significant control over their policy as their life circumstances change. At its core, universal life includes a savings component that earns interest monthly, with the interest rate adjusted periodically by the insurer, but usually with a guaranteed minimum rate. This cash value component grows tax-deferred and can be used during the policyholder's lifetime for any purpose, such as paying premiums, providing an emergency fund, or even supplementing retirement income. The flexibility to use the cash value distinguishes universal life from other permanent life insurance products and provides a valuable liquidity option not typically available with whole life insurance.

One of the most attractive features of universal life is the ability to modify premium payments within certain limits. Policyholders can choose to pay higher premiums when they have more disposable income or reduce or even eliminate payments during periods of financial stress, provided there is sufficient cash value to cover the cost of the policy. This can be particularly beneficial for people with fluctuating incomes or those who expect their financial situation to change significantly over time.

In addition, the death benefit of a universal life policy can be adjusted. Policyholders can choose to increase the death benefit as their financial responsibilities increase, such as the birth of a child or the purchase of a home, subject to insurability. Conversely, they can reduce the death benefit if they find they no longer need as much cover, which can also reduce the amount of premium they have to pay. This ability to tailor the death benefit to specific needs over time is a crucial advantage of universal life insurance, providing flexibility and security.

Universal life insurance also requires careful management. The performance of the policy can vary with interest rates, and managing the cash value requires attention to ensure it doesn't dwindle to a level where the policy could lapse. Therefore, policyholders must review their policies regularly with their advisers to make any necessary adjustments in response to economic conditions and personal circumstances. In addition, the cost transparency of universal life insurance is a notable advantage. Charges within the policy, such as administration fees and insurance costs, are usually broken down and listed, unlike whole life insurance, where costs may be embedded in the premium and not visible. This transparency allows for better financial planning and understanding of how one's money is used.

So, universal life offers an attractive blend of flexibility, growth potential, and transparency, making it ideal for savvy consumers who want to manage their financial instruments closely. It serves not only as a safety net but also as a dynamic financial resource that adapts to the evolving financial landscape of the insured, providing tailored solutions to meet complex and changing economic needs.

VARIABLE LIFE INSURANCE

Variable life insurance is a complex and versatile form of permanent life insurance that combines the protection of traditional life insurance with the growth potential of investment accounts. This type of policy can allocate cash values to various investment options, ranging from stocks and bonds to money market funds, offering policyholders the potential for higher returns based on market performance, albeit with increased risk. The foundation of variable life insurance is the death benefit, designed to provide financial security for beneficiaries during the policyholder's death. The flexibility it offers in investment choices sets variable life insurance apart. Policyholders can choose how to invest the policy's cash value from the separate account options available, each with its risk and return profile. This allows policyholders to tailor their investment strategy to their personal risk tolerance and financial goals, making it an attractive option for those knowledgeable about financial markets and comfortable with investment risk.

With a variable life insurance policy, premiums are fixed and part of the premium is invested in the life insurance policy, while the rest is invested in the chosen funds. The value of the cash account in a variable life insurance policy is not guaranteed and will fluctuate with the performance of the underlying investment options. As a result, the cash value of the policy, and possibly the death benefit, may rise or fall depending on the performance of the invested assets. This introduces a layer of investment risk, as poor market performance can reduce the cash value and, if not managed properly, may even require additional premiums to maintain the policy.

Despite this risk, the attraction of variable life is the potential for significant cash value growth in a favorable market environment. This growth is tax-deferred, providing an additional benefit as policyholders do not pay tax on any gains as long as they remain within the policy. In addition, policyholders can make tax-free withdrawals or borrow against the cash value, providing financial flexibility during the policyholder's lifetime. In addition, the investment flexibility within variable life policies can act as an inflation hedge, as the potential for higher returns can offset the declining purchasing power of a fixed death benefit. This makes variable life insurance a strategic component of broader financial planning, providing a death benefit and a mechanism for wealth accumulation and estate planning.

However, the complex nature of variable life insurance requires policyholders to remain informed and actively involved in managing their policies. Regular reviews with financial advisers are essential to adjust investment allocations as market conditions change and the policyholder's personal and financial circumstances evolve. This ongoing management is essential to ensure that the policy meets the policyholder's financial protection and investment objectives. Let's end this topic by saying that variable life insurance offers a unique combination of life insurance protection and investment potential, suitable for those knowledgeable about the markets and comfortable with investment risk. Its ability to provide tailored investment strategies within a life insurance policy makes it a sophisticated financial tool for managing long-term financial security and asset growth.

SURVIVORSHIP LIFE INSURANCE

Survivorship life insurance, also known as second-to-die life insurance, is a distinctive type of policy designed primarily for couples, particularly those interested in estate planning or providing for heirs with special needs. This policy covers two people under one agreement and pays out the death benefit only after the second insured person passes away. This unique setup makes survivorship life insurance an ideal tool for managing estate taxes and ensuring that heirs receive a legacy free from substantial tax burdens.

The core appeal of survivorship life insurance lies in its strategic application in estate planning. Often, estate taxes can significantly diminish the financial legacy left for heirs. Using a survivorship life insurance policy, a couple can ensure sufficient funds are available to cover these taxes and other estate-related expenses without the need to liquidate other assets. This is particularly advantageous for estates involving significant assets such as real estate or a family business, where premature liquidation could be financially disadvantageous or against the wishes of the surviving spouse or beneficiaries.

Moreover, premiums for survivorship life insurance are generally lower than those for two separate individual life insurance policies, primarily because the probability of both insured individuals dying within a short period is lower than the probability of either dying at a given time. This cost efficiency not only makes it accessible but also appealing to those who may be uninsurable on an individual basis due to health issues; however, when paired with a healthier spouse in a survivorship policy, they can still secure crucial coverage.

Survivorship life insurance also plays a significant role in charitable giving. For couples passionate about a charitable cause, the policy can be structured to provide a substantial donation upon their passing, thus leaving behind a meaningful legacy to a cause they support. This fulfills philanthropic goals and offers potential tax advantages that can further benefit the remaining estate.

The policy's flexibility in beneficiaries and its benefits extend beyond the immediate family. It can be used to secure inheritances for children from previous marriages or to fund trusts for dependents with special needs, ensuring that financial support continues throughout their lifetime without disrupting government aid.

Furthermore, the delayed payout characteristic of survivorship life insurance encourages long-term financial planning and investment, as the funds are not immediately required for survivor support but are intended for future use. This allows financial planners and policyholders to craft a comprehensive approach to wealth transfer, considering other investments and assets that will benefit the heirs directly. Survivorship life insurance remains a robust tool for estate planning, offering couples a strategic way to manage their financial legacy. Providing a mechanism to address estate taxes and facilitating the transfer of wealth to the next generation or charitable organizations ensures that the policyholders' financial goals and legacy intentions are realized.

GROUP LIFE INSURANCE

Group life insurance is an advantageous policy typically offered by employers, associations or large organizations as part of a benefits package to their employees or members. It provides life insurance cover for a group under a single master policy, simplifying administration and reducing costs compared to individual life insurance policies. This type of insurance is particularly valuable as a basic security measure for employees, providing them with an essential layer of financial protection and contributing to a more supportive and attractive working environment.

The primary appeal of group life is its inclusiveness and affordability. By spreading the risk across a group of individuals, the cost per member is significantly lower than if they were to purchase a similar amount of individual life insurance. This is a key benefit, particularly for employees who might not otherwise be able to afford life insurance due to high premiums or personal health issues. Group policies typically do not require individual members to provide evidence of insurability, which not only streamlines the enrolment process, but also allows individuals with pre-existing conditions to obtain coverage they might not be able to obtain on their own.

Employers often provide a basic level of coverage at no cost to the employee, with the option to purchase additional coverage through payroll deductions at group rates that are more affordable than individual rates. This structure makes group life insurance an excellent complement to personal life insurance policies, enhancing employees' overall benefits packages and providing more excellent coverage. In addition, for many employees, this benefit is automatic, meaning they receive some level of life insurance protection simply by their employment, without making any active decisions or allocations.

Group life insurance policies typically provide a death benefit based on the employee's salary, often one to two times the annual salary. While this amount may not meet all the long-term financial needs of the employee's beneficiaries, such as paying off a mortgage or funding higher education for dependents, it can provide significant immediate relief in covering funeral costs and other urgent expenses after a loss. For more comprehensive coverage, employees can often increase their coverage by paying additional premiums and tailoring the benefit to suit their individual needs and circumstances better.

Another important aspect of group life insurance is its portability. While leaving an employer traditionally means losing coverage, many modern group life policies allow employees to convert their group coverage to individual policies when they leave the company, retire or are terminated. Although premiums may increase upon conversion, the ability to maintain coverage without a medical exam provides an important safety net for those who may have health concerns.

Group life insurance also plays a key role in employee retention and morale. It is often seen as a symbol of an employer's investment in the well-being of its employees and their families. By offering life insurance as part of a comprehensive benefits package, employers help alleviate one of the most significant financial concerns employees may face, resulting in a more focused and engaged workforce. This insurance is an invaluable benefit that provides security and peace of mind to employees by giving basic life cover or acting as a supplement to individual life insurance policies. Its cost-effectiveness, ease of enrolment, and portability make it a critical component of employee benefit programs, enhancing an employer's attractiveness in a competitive labor market.

CONVERTIBLE POLICIES

Convertible life insurance policies offer a unique blend of flexibility and security, making them an attractive option for individuals anticipating changes in their financial situation or insurance needs. These policies are typically term life insurance plans that provide an option to convert into permanent life insurance without undergoing further medical underwriting, regardless of any changes in the policyholder's health. This feature is crucial for maintaining life insurance coverage when it might otherwise become unaffordable or unavailable due to deteriorating health.

Convertible policies cater primarily to those who initially opt for term life insurance because of its affordability and simplicity but who also appreciate the option to secure longer-term coverage if their needs change. The conversion feature allows policyholders to start with lower premium costs and then switch to a permanent policy, such as whole life or universal life, which provides lifelong coverage and builds cash value over time.

The ability to convert is particularly beneficial under several circumstances. For instance, a young professional without immediate financial responsibilities might choose a term policy due to lower premiums. As they age, marry, or start a family, their financial responsibilities increase, and the desire for a more permanent insurance solution grows. Here, the convertible policy provides security by maintaining continuous coverage.

Furthermore, the conversion process is designed to be straightforward, usually not requiring a medical exam or extensive paperwork, thus eliminating the worry that a change in health status could make insurance unaffordable or unattainable. This seamless transition is a significant relief to policyholders who might develop health conditions that could make them uninsurable under normal circumstances.

When considering a convertible policy, it's essential to be aware of the conversion period—this is the timeframe during which conversion is allowed. It's typically set before the term policy expires, and failing to convert within this period might result in losing the opportunity to do so without further health assessments. Policyholders should understand these details to plan their insurance strategy effectively. In essence, convertible policies provide a strategic insurance solution that supports individuals throughout different stages of life, adapting to their evolving financial and family circumstances. This adaptability ensures continued protection and enhances the long-term value of their initial insurance investment.

RIDERS AND ENDORSEMENTS

Riders and endorsements are additional provisions that can be added to a standard insurance policy to customize it better to meet the policyholder's personal needs or risk profile. These modifications can either expand or restrict the benefits provided, offering tailored insurance solutions that enhance the value and functionality of a life insurance policy.

Riders are particularly popular in life insurance because they allow policyholders to adjust coverage to align with their changing life circumstances or specific concerns without purchasing an entirely new policy. Common examples of riders include the waiver of premium rider, which forgives premium payments if the policyholder becomes disabled and unable to work; the accelerated death benefit rider, which allows policyholders to receive a portion of their death benefit early if they are diagnosed with a terminal illness; and the term conversion rider, which enables conversion from a term to a permanent policy.

Endorsements can also modify policies but are more often used to include exceptions or specific conditions that alter the standard coverage terms. Both riders and endorsements play a crucial role in personalizing life insurance policies, making them more flexible and responsive to individual needs.

Adding riders or endorsements typically involves additional premiums, reflecting the increased risk or expanded coverage the insurer must assume. However, the cost is often justified by the peace of mind and added protection these features offer. For example, adding a critical illness rider can provide financial relief in the event of severe health issues, ensuring that policyholders can access necessary funds for treatment without depleting their savings. Riders and endorsements enhance life insurance policies' adaptability and personal relevance. Allowing policyholders to customize their coverage ensures that insurance protection remains aligned with individual circumstances and priorities over time, providing financial security and a tailored approach to risk management.

POLICY LOANS AND WITHDRAWALS

Policy loans and withdrawals are features offered under many permanent life insurance policies, such as whole life and universal life insurance, that allow policyholders to access part of their policy's cash value without terminating the policy. This flexibility is one of the distinct advantages of permanent life insurance, providing financial options that can be pivotal during times of need.

A policy loan allows the policyholder to borrow money from the insurance company using the cash value of their life insurance policy as collateral. Unlike traditional loans from a financial institution, a policy loan typically does not require a credit check or a lengthy approval process, making it a convenient source of funds. The interest rates on policy loans are generally competitive with other types of personal loans, and since the loan is secured against the policy's cash value, it can often be obtained more quickly and with less procedural complexity.

One key advantage of policy loans is that they are not taxable as long as the policy remains in force. However, it's important to manage these loans carefully. Interest on the loan accrues, and if not repaid, it can compound and reduce the policy's death benefit and cash value. If the loan plus accumulated interest exceeds the policy's cash value, the policy could lapse, potentially leading to a significant tax liability if the withdrawn amount exceeds the premiums paid into the policy.

Policy Withdrawals

In addition to loans, many policies allow direct withdrawals from the cash value. Withdrawals reduce the cash value and death benefit directly and may have tax implications if the amount withdrawn exceeds the premiums paid into the policy. However, they do not accrue interest like loans do and provide a straightforward way to access funds.

Withdrawals are particularly useful for policyholders who need to cover immediate expenses, such as emergency medical costs, home repairs, or college tuition. Unlike loans, withdrawals do not need to be repaid. Still, because they reduce the death benefit, policyholders must consider how this will affect their long-term financial planning and the future security of their beneficiaries.

Strategic Use of Policy Loans and Withdrawals

For many, the ability to take loans or make withdrawals from a life insurance policy provides a financial safety net during periods of economic uncertainty. For example, during a market downturn, a policyholder might prefer to take a loan against their life insurance rather than sell off other investments at a loss. This strategic use of life insurance as a financial resource can provide significant flexibility and security, allowing policyholders to weather financial storms without disrupting their long-term investment strategy.

However, policyholders need to understand the implications of accessing cash value through loans and withdrawals. It is advisable to consult with a financial advisor to discuss how these actions might impact their overall financial strategy and the potential consequences for the policy and its beneficiaries. Responsible management ensures that the policy continues to provide the intended financial security and benefits for which it was originally purchased.

Dividends and bonuses in life insurance are features typically associated with participating whole life insurance policies. These features enhance the policy's value over time and offer policyholders a share in the insurance company's profits. As we conclude Chapter 2, understanding how dividends and bonuses work provides a solid foundation for managing a life insurance policy effectively and makes for a smooth transition into the practical applications of these concepts in Chapter 3.

Understanding Dividends and Bonuses

Dividends are essentially a return of excess premium payments and are paid out when the insurance company achieves better-than-expected financial performance, cost savings, or favorable claims experiences. Although dividends are not guaranteed, they are a valuable benefit for policyholders when they are distributed. Policyholders can choose to receive these dividends in cash, use them to reduce future premiums, accumulate them at interest, or purchase additional insurance coverage known as paid-up additions, which increase both the cash value and the death benefit of the policy.

Similar to dividends but more common in jurisdictions like the UK or India, Bonuses represent additional sums added to the benefit payable under the policy. These are declared annually and once added, they cannot be taken away. Bonuses increase the policy's maturity value and enhance the total life coverage, providing greater financial security to the beneficiaries.

The strategic value of dividends and bonuses lies in their ability to improve the policy's performance over time. For instance, reinvesting dividends into purchasing additional paid-up insurance increases the death benefit and accelerates the growth of the policy's cash value. This compounding effect can significantly enhance the financial leverage of the policy without requiring additional out-of-pocket premium payments from the policyholder.

These reinvestment options make participating whole life insurance an attractive long-term investment. The flexibility to use dividends to pay premiums can also be particularly appealing during times of financial strain, offering a buffer that can keep a policy active without additional financial burden on the policyholder.

As we move from the detailed exploration of life insurance types and their unique benefits in Chapter 2, Chapter 3 will delve into the practical applications of these policies. We will explore real-life scenarios where the strategic use of life insurance plays a pivotal role in financial planning, asset management, and legacy building. Whether leveraging cash values through loans and withdrawals, optimizing the economic impact of dividends and bonuses, or utilizing life insurance as a tool for estate planning, the next chapter will provide actionable insights that help readers make the most of their life insurance policies.

Thus, as you continue to navigate through the complexities of life insurance, the forthcoming chapter promises to equip you with the knowledge to apply these concepts effectively. The understanding of dividends and bonuses enhances your ability to manage your policy and prepares you to maximize the benefits these features can offer, aligning your financial goals with the mechanisms of your life insurance policy.

CHAPTER 3

HEALTH INSURANCE IN DETAIL

INDIVIDUAL HEALTH INSURANCE

Individual health insurance is a crucial option for self-employed people, those between jobs, or those employed at a workplace that does not offer group insurance. This type of policy allows individuals or families to tailor coverage directly to their health needs and financial situation, providing an essential safety net that covers medical expenses ranging from routine doctor visits to major surgeries.

When purchasing individual health insurance, policyholders can choose from various plans, each varying in cost, coverage level, and network of healthcare providers. The flexibility to select a plan that best suits one's health needs is a significant advantage of individual health insurance. Plans can range from basic coverage, typically covering only catastrophic events, to comprehensive plans that include preventive care, prescription drugs, mental health services, and maternity care.

Premiums for individual health insurance are determined based on several factors, including the policyholder's age, geographic location, tobacco use, and chosen plan category. Unlike group insurance, where the risk and cost are distributed among many employees, individual policy costs directly reflect the personal health risks and expected usage of the individual or family purchasing the insurance. Additionally, individuals with pre-existing conditions cannot be denied coverage or charged higher rates, which is a mandate of the Affordable Care Act (ACA). The ACA also introduced subsidies for individual health insurance, making it more affordable for many Americans. These subsidies are available to individuals and families with incomes between 100% and 400% of the federal poverty level and can significantly reduce the cost of premiums. Furthermore, the ACA established health insurance marketplaces, or exchanges, that facilitate comparing and purchasing health insurance plans, ensuring that consumers can evaluate different options and find one that best fits their budget and healthcare needs.

Another aspect of individual health insurance is the annual open enrollment period, during which individuals can enroll in a new health insurance plan or change their current plan. Special enrollment periods are also available for those who experience specific life events, such as getting married, having a baby, or losing other health coverage, allowing for adjustments outside the typical enrollment window.

In essence, individual health insurance provides vital medical coverage for those without access to group plans, offering diverse options to accommodate a range of healthcare needs and financial circumstances. With the ability to customize their coverage, individuals can ensure they have the necessary protection to manage their health effectively, maintaining their well-being and financial stability in the face of medical uncertainties.

GROUP HEALTH INSURANCE

Group health insurance is a critical component of employee benefits packages offered by many employers. This type of insurance pools together a group of employees, offering them medical coverage under one policy. Because the risk is shared among a group rather than an individual, group health insurance plans are generally more cost-effective for members, providing broader coverage at a lower cost per individual than would be possible with individual policies.

The essence of group health insurance lies in its ability to leverage the collective bargaining power of the group to negotiate better terms with insurance providers, including lower premiums and more comprehensive coverage options. This makes group health insurance particularly attractive to employees, as it often covers a wider range of medical services at a more affordable price. Employers typically contribute a significant portion of the premium costs, which not only helps to lower the financial burden on employees but also enhances job satisfaction and employee retention. Coverage under group health insurance typically extends to a variety of healthcare needs, including preventive services, emergency care, hospitalization, surgeries, and prescription medications. Many plans also offer added benefits such as dental, vision, and mental health services. Including preventive care is particularly beneficial, as it encourages employees to undertake regular health check-ups and screenings, which can lead to early detection and treatment of health issues, ultimately reducing overall healthcare costs for both employers and employees.

Enrollment in group health insurance is usually offered upon hiring, with employees required to opt in or out of coverage within a designated period. Additionally, there are annual open enrollment periods during which employees can make changes to their coverage, add or remove dependents, or switch between different plans offered by the employer. Special enrollment periods are also available for employees who experience significant life events, such as marriage, the birth of a child, or the loss of other medical coverage, allowing them to update their insurance coverage to reflect their new circumstances.

Furthermore, group health insurance plans are subject to regulations that protect the rights of employees. For instance, under the Health Insurance Portability and Accountability Act (HIPAA), employees and their families may have the right to special enrollment in other group health plans for which they are eligible if they lose their group health coverage, ensuring continuous protection against medical expenses.

Group health insurance is not just a benefit but a fundamental aspect of employment that enhances the well-being of employees. By providing cost-effective, comprehensive health coverage, group health insurance plays a pivotal role in supporting the physical and financial health of the workforce while also contributing to a positive organizational culture and aiding in the attraction and retention of top talent.

SHORT-TERM HEALTH INSURANCE

Short-term health insurance, often called temporary health insurance, is designed to provide coverage during gaps in traditional health insurance coverage. This type of insurance benefits individuals transitioning between jobs, recent college graduates, individuals waiting for employer benefits to start, or those who missed open enrollment periods for standard insurance plans. It offers a crucial safety net when individuals might otherwise be uninsured.

Short-term health insurance plans are typically available for durations ranging from one month to up to one year, depending on state regulations. In some states, these plans can be renewed for up to three years. The appeal of short-term insurance lies in its flexibility and immediacy; policies can often be implemented within days of application, providing rapid coverage that is essential in avoiding significant gaps in health insurance.

One of the primary characteristics of short-term health insurance is its streamlined application process. Unlike standard health insurance plans that require comprehensive medical questionnaires and can impose waiting periods for coverage to start, short-term plans often feature simplified underwriting processes that might not cover pre-existing conditions. This expedited underwriting allows for quick policy issuance, which is critical for those in immediate need of coverage.

However, the benefits of short-term health insurance come with certain limitations. These plans typically do not cover pre-existing conditions, which can be a significant drawback for individuals with ongoing medical needs. Additionally, the coverage provided is usually more limited than that of traditional health insurance plans. For instance, short-term plans may not cover maternity care, mental health services, or prescription drugs, and the coverage limits and deductibles can be substantially higher. Despite these limitations, short-term health insurance costs are generally lower than traditional plans, primarily because of the restricted coverage and the exclusion of pre-existing conditions. This cost-effectiveness makes short-term health insurance an attractive option for those in relatively good health and in need of temporary coverage.

Another aspect to consider is the regulatory environment surrounding short-term health insurance, which varies significantly by state. Some states have stringent regulations that restrict the sale of these plans. In contrast, others have embraced them as a viable option for consumers seeking temporary coverage. Consumers must understand the specific regulations and conditions of short-term health insurance in their state to ensure they are adequately covered. Short-term health insurance serves a unique and essential role in the healthcare insurance landscape. It provides an interim solution for health coverage that bridges the gap until more permanent insurance options can be secured. While it is not intended to replace long-term health insurance plans, its availability is crucial for providing immediate coverage in times of transition, protecting individuals from unforeseen medical costs and giving them peace of mind during periods of vulnerability. As such, while considering short-term health insurance, individuals must carefully assess their health needs, understand the specific terms and limitations of the policy, and consider how it fits within their broader health insurance strategy.

LONG-TERM HEALTH INSURANCE

Long-term health insurance is designed to cover the cost of care for individuals who can no longer perform basic daily activities due to chronic illness, disability, or advancing age. This type of insurance is critical as it covers services that are not typically provided by regular health insurance, Medicare, or Medicaid, such as extended stays in nursing facilities, home health care, and custodial care. As the population ages, the demand for long-term health insurance has increased significantly, reflecting the need for financial protection against the high costs associated with prolonged health care services.

Long-term health insurance plans can be tailored to a variety of coverage needs, from in-home care provided by a nurse or aide to full-time care in a licensed nursing facility. The benefits of these plans are typically activated when the insured person is certified as being unable to engage in a certain number of Activities of Daily Living (ADLs) independently, such as bathing, dressing, or eating. The specifics of what triggers benefits can vary between policies, but all are designed to offer peace of mind and financial security, ensuring that long-term care needs do not cause undue financial strain.

The policies can also differ in the length of time they will pay out benefits, from a few years to the remainder of a person's life, and in the daily or monthly benefit amounts. Some plans include inflation protection, which is highly recommended as the cost of care will likely increase over time. This feature ensures that the benefits provided keep pace with rising costs, preserving the policy's value and effectiveness.

Purchasing long-term health insurance requires careful consideration and planning. Buying a policy when younger and in good health is generally less expensive. Waiting until one is older or after a significant health diagnosis can make obtaining coverage more costly and complex. Moreover, individuals must evaluate their potential future health needs, family health history, and financial resources to choose a policy that best meets their anticipated needs.

DISABILITY INSURANCE

Disability insurance is a type of coverage designed to provide income if a worker cannot perform their job and earn an income due to a disability. This insurance is essential for individuals who depend heavily on their working income and offers financial protection by ensuring a continuous income stream during periods of disability. Policies can cover both short-term and long-term disabilities, ranging from a few months to lifelong coverage.

Disability insurance policies are typically categorized into two types: short-term disability (STD) and long-term disability (LTD) insurance. STD policies usually cover individuals from a few weeks to a year. LTD policies can extend from a few years up to retirement age. The money paid out in benefits is usually a percentage of the policyholder's regular income, commonly between 50% and 70%.

One of the significant benefits of disability insurance is that it covers not only disabilities stemming from accidents but also those that may result from various illnesses, making it a comprehensive safety net for physical and mental health challenges. This is particularly important as illnesses like cancer, heart attacks, and other severe conditions can unexpectedly hinder one's ability to work. Deciding when to purchase disability insurance is crucial. Ideally, individuals should consider acquiring it while they are still healthy, as pre-existing conditions can make it more difficult or more expensive to obtain coverage later. Additionally, many employers offer disability insurance as part of their benefits package, often at a lower group rate. However, it's essential to understand any employer-provided policy's specific terms and coverage limits to determine if additional private insurance is needed.

Disability insurance is an integral part of a comprehensive financial planning strategy, providing crucial income protection that helps individuals maintain their standard of living and meet financial obligations during periods when they cannot work due to disability. Understanding the different types of disability insurance and their benefits can empower individuals to make informed decisions about their insurance needs, ensuring they are well-protected against unexpected health issues' potentially devastating financial impact.

MEDICARE

Medicare is a federal health insurance program in the United States primarily designed for people aged 65 and older. However, it also covers younger individuals with specific disabilities and diseases, such as End-Stage Renal Disease and amyotrophic lateral sclerosis. Established in 1965, Medicare aims to address the health insurance needs of older Americans, ensuring they receive adequate medical care without the burden of prohibitive costs. Understanding Medicare's structure, benefits, and limitations is crucial for anyone approaching retirement age or those managing certain health conditions.

Medicare Structure

Medicare is divided into four parts, each designed to cover specific health-related services:

- **Part A (Hospital Insurance):** This part covers inpatient hospital stays, care in a skilled nursing facility, hospice care, and some home health care. Most people do not pay a premium for Part A if they or their spouse paid Medicare taxes while working. This is because they are considered "prepaid" via their payroll taxes over the years.

- **Part B (Medical Insurance):** Part B covers certain doctors' services, outpatient care, medical supplies, and preventive services. Unlike Part A, Part B requires a monthly premium that depends on the beneficiary's income, with most people paying a standard rate.

- **Part C (Medicare Advantage):** These are Medicare-approved plans offered by private companies that provide all of the benefits of Parts A and B. Many Medicare Advantage plans also include drug coverage (Part D) and other benefits like vision, dental, and hearing, often with additional premiums.

- **Part D (Prescription Drug Coverage):** This part covers the cost of prescription drugs, including many recommended shots or vaccines. Part D plans are also offered by Medicare-approved private companies.

Enrollment and Eligibility

Individuals are typically eligible for Medicare at 65, although those with qualifying disabilities may enroll earlier. The initial enrollment period begins three months before the month of one's 65th birthday and extends three months after. During this time, individuals can sign up for Medicare Part A and Part B. Failure to enroll during this period can lead to penalties, particularly for Part B, unless the individual is still working and covered by a group health plan.

Medicare Costs

While Medicare covers many health services, it does not cover all expenses. For example, long-term care is not covered by Medicare; there are also deductibles and copayments for many services. To help cover additional costs, many individuals purchase Medigap insurance, supplemental insurance from a private company that pays for costs not covered by Medicare, such as copayments, coinsurance, and deductibles.

Medicare and Medicaid

It's important to note the difference between Medicare and Medicaid. While Medicare is primarily for people over 65 and those with disabilities, Medicaid is an assistance program serving low-income people of all ages. Some individuals qualify for both programs and are known as "dual eligibles." They can receive coverage for additional services not covered by Medicare, such as long-term personal care services.

Impact and Importance

Medicare plays a crucial role in the health and financial stability of over 60 million Americans. It allows older adults and people with disabilities to receive necessary medical treatments without the crippling financial burdens that often accompany aging and illness. As healthcare costs continue to rise, Medicare's role in public health and its impact on the economy continues to grow, making it a critical element of national health policy.

For many, understanding Medicare is crucial in planning for healthcare in later life or in managing disabilities. It provides a foundation of coverage that can be supplemented with additional insurance to meet personal health needs, ensuring that individuals can access care without undue financial hardship.

Medicaid is a vital public assistance program in the United States that provides health coverage to millions of Americans, including eligible low-income adults, children, pregnant women, elderly adults, and people with disabilities. Jointly funded by the state and federal governments, it is administered at the state level, which allows for considerable variability in the coverage and services provided across different states. Understanding Medicaid is crucial for those who are potentially eligible, as it can significantly reduce the financial burden of medical expenses and increase access to necessary healthcare services.

Medicaid Eligibility and Coverage

Eligibility for Medicaid is primarily based on income, and the program is designed to assist those with the greatest economic need. The Affordable Care Act (ACA) expanded Medicaid eligibility in many states to include all adults with incomes up to 138% of the federal poverty level, although not all states have chosen to expand their Medicaid programs. Besides financial criteria, eligibility can also depend on other factors such as family size, pregnancy, disability status, and other special conditions.

Medicaid covers a broad range of health services, typically including hospitalization, laboratory services, x-rays, doctor services, and more. For children, Medicaid coverage extends to the Early and Periodic Screening, Diagnostic, and Treatment (EPSDT) service, which includes regular check-ups and necessary medical treatments. Furthermore, Medicaid provides comprehensive coverage that includes services not always covered by Medicare, such as long-term care in nursing facilities and personal care services.

Impact of Medicaid

Medicaid serves as a lifeline for many low-income families, individuals with disabilities, and elderly people who may not have access to affordable healthcare otherwise. It plays a critical role in improving health outcomes by providing preventive care, chronic disease management, and medical treatments that recipients might not otherwise afford. Studies have shown that Medicaid expansion under the ACA has led to increased health insurance coverage, improved health outcomes, and reduced mortality rates.

Medicaid and State Flexibility

Since the states administer Medicaid, there is significant variation in how services are delivered and what is covered. This state flexibility allows programs to be tailored to meet the needs of the local population but can also lead to disparities in access and quality of care across state lines. States can expand their Medicaid programs with federal funding, yet some states have opted not to expand their coverage, leaving many low-income adults without health insurance options.

Challenges and Considerations

Despite its benefits, Medicaid faces several challenges, including budget constraints, varying state policies, and sometimes limited provider participation due to lower reimbursement rates compared to private insurance or Medicare. These factors can impact the quality and accessibility of care for Medicaid beneficiaries. Additionally, navigating Medicaid's application and renewal processes can be complex, requiring applicants to provide detailed documentation about their income, family size, and more.

Future of Medicaid

As healthcare needs evolve and the population ages, Medicaid continues to adapt. Ongoing debates around healthcare policy in the U.S. often focus on how best to manage and fund Medicaid, balancing cost with the need to provide comprehensive and accessible healthcare. The program's flexibility allows it to respond to public health crises, such as the COVID-19 pandemic, during which Medicaid quickly adapted to provide necessary coverage for millions affected by the crisis.

Medicaid not only supports the health of millions of Americans but also provides economic benefits by reducing unpaid medical bills and supporting healthcare providers. For many, it is an essential program that promotes public health and financial stability, making understanding and maintaining this program vital for the wellbeing of many Americans.

SUPPLEMENTAL HEALTH INSURANCE

Supplemental health insurance is designed to complement primary health insurance policies by covering additional costs that regular insurance may not fully cover. This type of insurance can be crucial for managing out-of-pocket expenses such as copayments, deductibles, and coinsurance, which can accumulate significantly, especially in the event of unexpected medical issues or accidents. Supplemental health insurance can encompass a range of specific policies, including critical illness insurance, accidental death and dismemberment insurance, and hospital indemnity insurance, among others. Understanding the nuances and benefits of supplemental health insurance can greatly enhance one's overall healthcare strategy, ensuring more comprehensive financial protection against health-related expenses.

Role and Importance of Supplemental Health Insurance

The primary role of supplemental health insurance is to fill the gaps left by standard health insurance plans. Many individuals find that while their primary health insurance covers a substantial portion of healthcare costs, the associated out-of-pocket expenses can still pose financial challenges. Supplemental insurance policies help alleviate these financial burdens by providing additional coverage for specific areas that are only partially covered or not covered by standard health plans.

For instance, critical illness insurance provides a lump-sum cash benefit upon the diagnosis of certain severe illnesses listed in the policy, such as cancer, heart attack, or stroke. This benefit can be used at the discretion of the insured to cover high deductibles, out-of-network specialists, travel and lodging for treatment, or even non-medical bills, ensuring that the financial impact of a critical illness doesn't compound the physical and emotional stress experienced during such times.

Benefits and Features

One of the significant benefits of supplemental health insurance is its flexibility. The payouts are typically made directly to the policyholder rather than to healthcare providers, giving recipients the freedom to use the funds where they are most needed. This aspect can be particularly beneficial when managing the indirect costs of illness, such as lost income or additional childcare expenses, which are not typically covered by standard health insurance.

Supplemental policies are also known for their ease of use. They often have straightforward eligibility criteria, simplified underwriting processes, and quick disbursement of benefits. These features make supplemental insurance an accessible option for many individuals seeking additional coverage.

Target Audience

Supplemental health insurance is particularly valuable for individuals who face high health risks or financial exposure due to their family medical history or nature of their employment. For example, individuals in high-risk professions may benefit from accidental death and dismemberment policies, while those with a family history of major illnesses might find critical illness insurance especially beneficial.

Additionally, as medical costs continue to rise, even those with robust primary health insurance coverage may find supplemental health insurance an essential component of their overall health coverage strategy, providing peace of mind that they can afford the necessary care without jeopardizing their financial stability.

Economic and Practical Considerations

From an economic perspective, the relatively low cost of supplemental insurance premiums compared to the potentially high cost of uncovered medical expenses can make these policies a prudent investment. Supplemental health insurance can contribute significantly to one's financial health by reducing potential debt from medical bills and protecting savings.

Moreover, in broader healthcare and insurance strategies, supplemental health insurance allows individuals to personalize their coverage to match their specific health needs and financial capabilities. This customization is critical in today's diverse healthcare landscape, where personal circumstances vary widely and one-size-fits-all solutions are often inadequate.

Overall Impact

Supplemental health insurance enhances healthcare coverage by providing financial resources that help bridge the gap between what primary insurance covers and the total cost of care. Its role in safeguarding policyholders from unexpected medical expenses and contributing to comprehensive health coverage make it a valuable component of health insurance planning. For many, investing in supplemental health insurance is not just a strategic financial decision but a crucial step toward ensuring complete and accessible healthcare coverage.

HEALTH MAINTENANCE ORGANIZATIONS (HMOs)

Health Maintenance Organizations (HMOs) represent a foundational structure in managed health care systems in the United States, emphasizing preventive care and integrated health services to improve health outcomes and reduce healthcare costs. As one of the most prevalent forms of managed care, HMOs require policyholders to receive care from a network of designated healthcare providers and facilities. This structure aims to foster a closer relationship between patients and their primary care providers, who act as gatekeepers to specialized services, ensuring that the care delivered is necessary, coordinated, and efficient.

Core Features of HMOs

The primary feature of HMO plans is the requirement for enrollees to select a primary care physician (PCP) from the HMO's network. This PCP is the patient's main healthcare provider and is responsible for managing all aspects of the patient's healthcare. If specialist consultation or treatment is required, the PCP will provide a referral within the HMO network, maintaining a coordinated approach to patient care. This model helps to streamline processes, reduce unnecessary tests or procedures, and focus on a continuity of care that is both proactive and preventive.

Cost-Effectiveness and Efficiency

HMOs are known for their cost-effectiveness, primarily due to the capitated payment system where doctors and hospitals are paid a fixed amount per enrollee, not based on the number of services provided. This payment method incentivizes providers to focus on maintaining the health of their patients to prevent illnesses and reduce the need for extensive medical services. Additionally, HMOs often have lower premiums and copayments than other insurance models, making them an attractive option for individuals and families seeking comprehensive health coverage without high out-of-pocket expenses.

Network Restrictions and Considerations

While HMOs offer numerous benefits, they also have limitations concerning provider networks. Enrollees must receive care from providers within the HMO's network, except in emergencies. This can be restrictive if preferred doctors or specialists are not in the network or if the network does not offer as wide a choice of providers as other types of health plans. For individuals who frequently travel or live in rural areas, the network limitations of an HMO might pose significant challenges.

Preventive Health Emphasis

A distinctive advantage of HMOs is their strong emphasis on preventive health care. These plans often include regular check-ups, screenings, and health education programs at little or no additional cost. The rationale is that long-term health care costs can be significantly reduced by investing in prevention. This proactive approach helps catch potentially serious health issues early on and aligns with a broader public health goal of reducing the incidence and impact of chronic diseases.

Choosing an HMO requires careful consideration of one's health care needs and preferences. For those who appreciate having a single point of contact for health concerns and who value the simplicity and predictability of the cost structure, an HMO can be an excellent choice. However, for those who require specialized care or who value flexibility in choosing providers, the restrictive nature of HMOs might be a drawback.

HMOs have profoundly impacted the structure and delivery of health care in the U.S. by providing an integrated care model emphasizing cost control, provider collaboration, and patient engagement. This model supports sustainable healthcare delivery and advances quality outcomes by fostering consistent and coordinated care. As the healthcare landscape continues to evolve, HMOs will likely play a crucial role in shaping future healthcare policies and practices, promoting a healthcare system that effectively balances cost, quality, and access to meet diverse patient needs.

PREFERRED PROVIDER ORGANIZATIONS (PPOs)

Preferred Provider Organizations (PPOs) are a popular type of health insurance plan that offer a higher degree of flexibility compared to Health Maintenance Organizations (HMOs). PPOs provide policyholders with a broad network of healthcare providers and allow them to choose specialists and healthcare services without needing primary care physician (PCP) referrals. This flexibility makes PPOs appealing to those who desire direct access to a wide range of medical professionals and facilities.

Structure and Functionality

PPOs operate through a network of designated healthcare providers who have agreed to provide medical services to members at negotiated lower rates. These networks include a wide array of specialists, hospitals, clinics, and primary care physicians, giving policyholders a variety of choices when it comes to their healthcare needs. One of the defining features of a PPO plan is that while it encourages members to use the network providers through lower copays and deductibles, it also offers the freedom to seek care outside of the network. However, receiving care from providers outside the network usually involves higher out-of-pocket costs, which is a key consideration for policyholders.

Financial Aspects

Regarding cost, PPOs generally have higher premiums than HMOs due to their greater flexibility. Despite the higher premium costs, many individuals and families find the additional expense justifiable for the freedom it provides in choosing healthcare providers. Moreover, PPOs typically involve deductibles and copayments, which the insured must pay out-of-pocket costs before the insurance covers the services. These plans often also have an out-of-pocket maximum, which can protect policyholders from very high medical expenses in a given year.

Benefits of PPOs

The main benefit of a PPO is its flexibility in allowing enrollees to visit any healthcare provider without a referral, which can significantly streamline the process of getting specialized care. This is especially beneficial for individuals with conditions that require frequent consultation with various specialists. Additionally, PPOs are advantageous for those who travel often or live in multiple locations, as they can receive care from various providers nationwide without worrying about staying within a specific network.

Considerations and Suitability

Choosing a PPO requires weighing several factors, including the higher cost of premiums against the need for flexibility and frequent access to healthcare services. A PPO plan can offer the right balance of flexibility and coverage for individuals who value choosing their medical providers and do not want to deal with the restrictions of needing referrals to see specialists. It's also well-suited for those who prefer having a safety net for out-of-network services, should they choose to receive care from providers not covered by the preferred network.

Impact on Healthcare Choices

PPOs profoundly impact personal healthcare management by providing a structure that supports individual preferences and needs. This model empowers consumers to make healthcare decisions that best suit their circumstances, promoting patient satisfaction and engagement in their health care journeys. As healthcare continues to evolve, the role of PPOs remains crucial in offering a compelling blend of flexibility, coverage, and controlled costs, making it a preferred choice for many seeking comprehensive health insurance options.

CHAPTER 4

INSURANCE REGULATIONS

STATE VS. FEDERAL REGULATION

Understanding the interplay between state and federal regulations in the insurance industry is crucial for professionals in the field. Insurance in the United States is primarily regulated at the state level, which allows for tailored approaches that consider local market conditions and consumer needs. However, federal regulations also play a significant role in enforcing nationwide standards and filling regulatory gaps that state laws may not address.

State Regulation

Each state has its own insurance department that is responsible for overseeing all insurance operations within its borders. This includes licensing insurers, regulating policy standards and claims practices, and ensuring the solvency of insurance companies. State regulators also handle consumer complaints and enforce local insurance laws that protect policyholders. The localized nature of state regulation allows for flexibility and adaptability to specific state needs but can also lead to a patchwork of regulations that vary significantly from one state to another.

State insurance departments actively monitor the insurers to ensure they comply with state statutes and regulations. This oversight includes reviewing rates and policy forms, conducting financial examinations, and auditing market practices. Additionally, states can impose penalties, including fines or license revocations, to enforce compliance.

Federal Regulation

While insurance is predominantly a state-regulated industry, federal oversight comes into play in certain areas. Notable examples include the Health Insurance Portability and Accountability Act (HIPAA), which sets standards for protecting sensitive patient data, and the Affordable Care Act (ACA), which has broad implications for health insurance coverage standards across the country.

Federal regulations often focus on areas where there's a need for uniformity across states or where interstate commerce is significantly affected. The federal government also steps in to regulate aspects of insurance that may impact national economic stability and the operation of large multinational insurers.

Interaction Between State and Federal Regulations

The interaction between state and federal regulations can sometimes lead to conflicts or overlapping authorities. For instance, while states are the primary regulators of insurance solvency and consumer protection, federal initiatives like the Dodd-Frank Wall Street Reform and Consumer Protection Act have increased federal involvement in insurance, especially in the oversight of systemic risk and the stability of large, internationally active insurers.

The National Association of Insurance Commissioners (NAIC) plays a key role in balancing state and federal regulations. The NAIC develops model laws and regulations aiming to create a degree of uniformity that can be adopted by individual states, helping to standardize certain regulatory aspects across state lines while respecting the state-based nature of insurance regulation.

Understanding the nuances of state versus federal regulation is essential for anyone involved in the insurance industry. It requires a keen awareness of the regulatory landscape, including ongoing legislative changes and how they impact insurance practices and policyholder rights. This knowledge is vital for effectively navigating and complying with the complex and often changing regulations that govern the insurance industry.

STATE-SPECIFIC REQUIREMENTS

Understanding and preparing for state-specific requirements is essential to studying for the Life and Health Insurance License Exam. Insurance laws and regulations can vary significantly from state to state, reflecting differences in legal frameworks, market practices, and consumer protection standards. These variations mean that candidates must not only master general insurance principles but also the specific rules and regulations applicable in the state where they intend to practice. This dual focus ensures that insurance professionals are well-prepared to pass their licensing exams and operate effectively and legally within their chosen locales.

Importance of State-Specific Knowledge

The decentralized nature of insurance regulation in the United States necessitates that insurance professionals thoroughly understand their state's specific legal and regulatory environment. This knowledge is crucial for passing the licensing exam and day-to-day operations, where professionals must navigate state-specific filing requirements, consumer complaint processes, and compliance regulations. In addition, understanding these unique requirements is vital for advising clients accurately and offering effective and legally sound solutions within the state.

Navigating State Regulations

Each state's insurance department typically publishes a set of guidelines and statutes that govern the licensing process and the conduct of insurance business within its jurisdiction. These documents are indispensable resources for anyone preparing for the state-specific portions of their exams. They detail everything from pre-licensing education requirements to ethical standards and are often accompanied by study materials or references to approved courses that can help candidates prepare effectively.

Furthermore, many states require that candidates complete a certain number of hours in state-approved training courses before sitting for the exam. These courses are designed to cover the national basics of insurance practice and the nuances of the state's insurance laws. Completing these education requirements is usually a prerequisite for qualifying for the licensing exam.

Study Strategies for State-Specific Exams

To effectively prepare for state-specific exam sections, candidates should invest time in study resources that are tailored to their state's exam. This might include state-issued manuals, courses offered by local colleges or professional training organizations, and practice tests that include state-specific questions. Engaging with local professional groups or networks can also provide insights and advice on the state exam's focus areas and difficulty level.

Additionally, many find it beneficial to create comparative charts or summaries that outline how their state's regulations differ from federal guidelines or standards in other states where they may have previous experience. This method helps isolate the unique aspects of the state's insurance landscape, making targeted study easier and more effective.

Practical Application and Continuing Education

After passing the exam, understanding state-specific requirements plays a crucial role in an insurance professional's career. States often require ongoing continuing education to maintain an insurance license, which keeps professionals up-to-date on changes in laws and regulations. Staying informed through these courses helps professionals avoid legal pitfalls and provides them with the latest information to serve their clients effectively.

A nuanced understanding of state-specific requirements is not just a stepping stone to obtaining a license; it is a fundamental aspect of professional practice in the insurance industry. By thoroughly preparing for these state-specific elements of the Life and Health Insurance License Exam, candidates ensure that they are ready not only to meet the immediate challenge of the exam but also to embrace the broader responsibilities of their roles as trusted insurance professionals.

When preparing for the Life and Health Insurance License Exam, it's crucial to consider the state-specific requirements that can vary significantly from one state to another. Below are unique requirements for the five states with the highest demand for this exam: California, Texas, Florida, New York, and Illinois. Each state has particular rules and educational prerequisites that candidates must fulfill to sit for the exam and practice as licensed insurance professionals.

California

California's insurance licensing requirements are stringent, reflecting the state's diverse demographics and unique geographical challenges, such as earthquakes and wildfires.

Candidates must complete a comprehensive 52-hour pre-licensing education, including 40 hours focused on general insurance principles and an additional 12 hours dedicated to ethics and the specifics of the California Insurance Code. This education is designed to prepare candidates thoroughly for a wide range of situations specific to California's insurance market.

The California insurance exam is tailored to reflect these state-specific nuances, particularly emphasizing areas like earthquake and wildfire insurance, which are of significant importance given the state's susceptibility to these natural disasters. Candidates are tested not only on general insurance knowledge but also on their understanding of California's detailed consumer protection laws, which are among the most robust in the nation. For instance, California has unique provisions regarding the disclosure of policy terms and handling claims post-natural disasters, which are crucial for effectively serving the state's policyholders.

Texas

In Texas, the pre-licensing education requirement consists of 40 hours that cover a broad spectrum of topics, from life and health insurance concepts to state-specific regulations. This requirement underscores Texas's commitment to ensuring that its insurance professionals are well-prepared to serve one of the largest insurance markets in the United States.

Texas's exam significantly emphasizes group health insurance plans and workers' compensation rules, reflecting the state's large industrial and service sectors. Texas also has specific regulations related to windstorm insurance, especially critical along its Gulf Coast. The exam tests candidates' knowledge on how these regional challenges affect insurance policies and consumer rights, ensuring that licensed agents are equipped to handle the particularities of insurance practices in Texas.

Florida

Florida requires its life and health insurance exam candidates to undertake 60 hours of pre-licensing education, reflecting the state's complex insurance environment influenced by its elderly population and high risk of hurricanes. The education covers standard insurance principles while emphasizing Florida-specific issues such as hurricane-related claims and the intricacies of flood insurance, a common concern in this hurricane-prone state.

The Florida insurance exam is notable for its detailed questions on insurance regulations concerning senior citizens, who comprise a significant portion of the state's population. Florida has specific laws designed to protect the elderly in insurance markets, including provisions against misleading practices in the sale of Medicare supplements and long-term care insurance. The state's exam ensures that professionals know these protective measures and can competently advise and support Florida's aging population.

New York

New York mandates 40 hours of pre-licensing education, including a detailed overview of state-specific insurance laws and practices. Given New York's status as a global financial hub, the state's insurance exam is particularly detailed, covering aspects of both local and international insurance regulations. The state also strongly emphasizes financial solvency and ethical standards, reflecting the complex interactions of various financial sectors within the state. The New York exam includes specific segments focusing on the state's unique no-fault auto insurance system and its implications for health insurance claims. It also covers local rules governing life insurance and annuity products, highlighting New York's consumer protection laws designed to safeguard the state's diverse and often densely populated communities.

Illinois

Illinois requires 20 hours of pre-licensing education for each major line of authority, with a portion of this education conducted in an interactive environment to foster a deeper understanding of the material. The state's exam focuses heavily on consumer protection laws and ethical insurance practices to ensure that agents fully understand their responsibilities to policyholders. The Illinois insurance exam rigorously tests knowledge on state-specific regulations, including detailed questions about Illinois' life and health insurance guarantees laws. This includes understanding the Illinois Health Insurance Portability and Accountability Act, which has specific provisions beyond the federal HIPAA rules, tailored to enhance the privacy and security of Illinois residents' health information.

Pennsylvania

In Pennsylvania, candidates aiming to become licensed insurance professionals must complete pre-licensing education tailored to ensure a deep understanding of national insurance principles and state-specific regulations. The state mandates 24 hours of pre-licensing education, with three hours dedicated to ethics. This training is designed to cover a broad spectrum of topics relevant to the diverse needs of Pennsylvania's population, including its large elderly demographic and significant rural areas. The Pennsylvania insurance exam focuses extensively on the state's specific provisions regarding annuities, long-term care, and Medicare supplemental policies. Given Pennsylvania's demographic profile, these are critical areas where insurance professionals must be knowledgeable. The state also has particular regulations concerning handling claims and consumer complaints, reflecting its consumer protection framework. Agents in Pennsylvania must be well-versed in understanding local flood insurance requirements, particularly in flood-prone areas, and how state laws interact with federal flood insurance policies. The exam ensures that all professionals are prepared to offer accurate and comprehensive advice to their clients, addressing both common and unique insurance needs within the state.

Ohio

Ohio requires its prospective insurance agents to complete 40 hours of pre-licensing education, focusing on various topics that reflect the state's industrial and agricultural diversity. This education prepares candidates for a comprehensive state exam that tests knowledge of Ohio-specific insurance laws and practical applications in real-world scenarios. Ohio's insurance exam places a particular emphasis on agricultural and commercial insurance, sectors that are vital to the state's economy. Candidates must demonstrate a thorough understanding of the specific needs and challenges associated with insuring agricultural operations and businesses, including equipment, livestock, and crop insurance. Furthermore, Ohio places a strong emphasis on ethics and fair consumer practices. The state's regulations are stringent regarding the disclosure of policy terms and the handling of claims, ensuring that insurance professionals maintain high standards of integrity and transparency in their dealings with clients. The exam tests for detailed knowledge of these regulations to ensure that agents are fully prepared to uphold the state's standards.

Georgia

Georgia requires insurance candidates to undergo 40 hours of pre-licensing education, including detailed modules on the specific risks associated with the state's geographical and economic characteristics, such as coastal storm impacts and large metropolitan area liabilities. The Georgia insurance exam is tailored to test candidates on their knowledge of local regulations affecting health insurance, particularly in how they apply to large employers in the state's growing industries. Additionally, Georgia has specific laws regarding the management of insurance premiums and the solvency of insurance companies, which are crucial for maintaining the financial stability of the insurance sector within the state.

Insurance professionals in Georgia are expected to be adept at navigating the complexities of property and casualty insurance, given the state's susceptibility to hurricanes and flooding. The exam rigorously tests knowledge in these areas to ensure agents are prepared to provide informed, accurate advice to property owners and businesses.

North Carolina

North Carolina's insurance licensing process includes completing pre-licensing education that focuses heavily on the state's diverse insurance needs—from rural agricultural insurance to urban property and casualty insurance. Candidates must complete 40 hours of education tailored to provide a comprehensive overview of these varying requirements. The North Carolina insurance exam emphasizes understanding state-specific auto, homeowners, and life insurance regulations. Given the state's exposure to hurricanes and other natural disasters, there is also a strong focus on disaster recovery and insurance claims processes related to natural disasters. North Carolina places particular importance on ethics and professional responsibility in the insurance industry. The state exam tests candidates' ability to handle ethical dilemmas and consumer protection issues effectively, ensuring they can serve North Carolina's policyholders with integrity.

Michigan

In Michigan, candidates are required to complete 40 hours of pre-licensing education, which includes an in-depth study of Michigan's no-fault automobile insurance system, one of the most complex in the United States. This system has specific requirements and benefits that are crucial for insurance professionals to understand. The Michigan insurance exam tests candidates on a wide range of topics, focusing on auto insurance, health insurance, and the integration of state and federal insurance regulations. Given Michigan's significant automotive industry, the state also highly emphasizes insurance products related to automotive manufacturing and liability. Michigan's approach to health insurance, especially concerning its Medicaid expansion and management under the Affordable Care Act, is another critical area of focus in the exam. Candidates must know how these policies affect insurers and insureds, ensuring comprehensive coverage and protection for consumers across the state.

These detailed preparations ensure that insurance professionals across these states are well-equipped to handle the specific insurance needs of their regions, fostering a well-regulated, effective, and consumer-oriented insurance market.

NAIC MODEL LAWS

The National Association of Insurance Commissioners (NAIC) plays a pivotal role in shaping the insurance regulatory landscape across the United States. Established as a standard-setting and regulatory support organization, the NAIC comprises the chief insurance regulators from each of the 50 U.S. states, the District of Columbia, and five U.S. territories. The NAIC's primary mission is to promote consistent and effective insurance regulation, facilitate the equitable treatment of insurance consumers, and maintain stable insurance markets. One of the key mechanisms through which the NAIC achieves these goals is the development and promotion of model laws and regulations.

Purpose and Impact of NAIC Model Laws

NAIC model laws serve as templates or benchmarks that individual state legislatures can adopt or adapt to enhance their insurance regulations. These models are crafted to address various issues within the insurance industry, including market conduct, company solvency, consumer protection, and health insurance standards. By providing a harmonized set of guidelines, the NAIC model laws help reduce regulatory discrepancies between states, facilitating a more uniform regulatory environment that benefits insurers and insureds.

Adopting model laws by states is not mandatory; however, the models are highly influential and widely regarded as best practices. Many states adopting these models create a de facto national standard without federal legislation. This approach respects the traditional state-based system of insurance regulation in the U.S. while promoting greater consistency across state lines, which is particularly important for insurance companies that operate in multiple states.

Examples of Key NAIC Model Laws

Some notable NAIC model laws include the Model Insurance Holding Company System Regulatory Act, which provides a framework for the regulation of insurance company groups; the Unfair Trade Practices Act, which addresses deceptive and unfair practices in the insurance marketplace; and the Life Insurance and Annuities Replacement Model Regulation, which protects consumers from potential disadvantages of replacing existing life insurance policies or annuities.

The Development Process

Developing NAIC model laws involves extensive collaboration among state insurance regulators, industry representatives, consumer advocates, and other stakeholders. This collaborative approach ensures that the models reflect a balanced perspective, addressing the needs and concerns of all parties involved in the insurance process. Once developed, these models undergo rigorous review and revision cycles to adapt to emerging trends and challenges in the insurance industry.

Strategic Importance of NAIC Model Laws

For insurance professionals, understanding the laws of the NAIC model is crucial. These laws influence current regulatory practices and guide the future direction of insurance regulation. Professionals knowledgeable about these models can better anticipate regulatory changes, manage compliance more effectively, and engage in advocacy efforts to influence future legislation.

NAIC model laws are foundational to fostering a cooperative regulatory environment that promotes effective oversight, consumer protection, and industry stability. They play a crucial role in shaping the standards that govern the U.S. insurance industry, making them essential knowledge for anyone involved in the insurance field.

MARKET CONDUCT

Market conduct within the insurance industry refers to the behavior and practices of insurers in their dealings with policyholders, claimants, and the overall public. It encompasses all aspects of the insurance lifecycle, including the marketing and selling of policies, underwriting, the handling of premiums, the provision of services, and the management of claims and complaints. Effective regulation of market conduct is essential to maintaining consumer trust, ensuring fair treatment, and fostering a competitive and stable insurance market.

Significance of Market Conduct Regulation

Market conduct regulation serves several key functions in the insurance industry. Firstly, it helps to ensure that insurers operate on a level playing field, where rules are clear and consistently applied, preventing anti-competitive practices. Secondly, it protects consumers from unfair or deceptive practices that could undermine their rights or financial interests. Finally, it enhances the overall stability and reputation of the insurance market by promoting transparency and accountability in insurers' operations.

Regulators focus on market conduct to prevent practices that might lead to consumer harm. This includes using misleading sales tactics, improper denial of claims, and discrimination in underwriting and pricing. State insurance departments conduct regular market conduct examinations to assess whether companies comply with applicable regulations and standards of practice.

Components of Market Conduct

Market conduct encompasses a wide range of insurer activities. In marketing and sales, regulators examine how insurance products are advertised and sold to the public. This includes reviewing advertising materials for accuracy and fairness and examining sales practices to ensure they are not misleading or coercive. In underwriting and pricing, market conduct involves ensuring that insurers use fair and equitable criteria to select and rate policyholders. This includes making sure that pricing structures do not discriminate against particular groups of people and that underwriting decisions are based on sound actuarial principles.

Claims processing is another critical area of market conduct regulation. Regulators monitor how insurers handle claims to ensure they are processed and paid out promptly and fairly. This includes reviewing procedures for investigating and assessing claims and policies for dispute resolution.

Enforcement of Market Conduct Standards

When violations of market conduct regulations are identified, regulatory bodies have several tools to enforce compliance. These can include imposing fines, limiting business practices, and in severe cases, withdrawing an insurer's license. Enforcement actions are punitive and serve as a deterrent against poor practices across the industry.

Challenges in Market Conduct Regulation

Regulating market conduct presents several challenges. The complexity of insurance products and the diversity of practices across different companies and jurisdictions make it difficult to create and enforce uniform standards. Additionally, the rapid evolution of the insurance industry, particularly with new technologies and distribution channels, continuously introduces new regulatory challenges.

Moreover, ensuring that regulation keeps pace with innovation without stifling growth is a delicate balance for regulators. They must be vigilant against new forms of consumer harm without imposing undue burdens on industry innovation and efficiency.

Impact of Effective Market Conduct Regulation

Effective market conduct regulation is vital for the health of the insurance industry. It builds consumer confidence by ensuring that insurance products and services are delivered fairly and transparently. For insurance companies, robust market conduct standards help to mitigate risks and avoid the costs associated with non-compliance, such as fines and reputational damage.

So, market conduct is a fundamental aspect of the insurance regulatory framework, essential for protecting consumers and maintaining the integrity of the insurance market. As the industry continues to evolve, so will the strategies and policies governing market conduct, requiring ongoing vigilance and adaptation by insurers and regulators.

CUSTOMER PROTECTION

Consumer protection in the insurance industry is essential for safeguarding policyholder rights and maintaining trust in the sector. It encompasses regulations and practices designed to ensure fair treatment from insurance companies, agents, and brokers throughout the customer journey—from advertising and purchasing to claims handling and dispute resolution. Regulatory bodies, primarily at the state level, enforce laws that protect consumers from unfair practices such as misleading advertisements, fraud, and unjust claim denials. A crucial element of consumer protection is the requirement for insurers to provide clear, accurate information about their products, including detailed disclosures about policy terms, benefits, exclusions, and costs in an understandable manner. This transparency helps consumers make informed decisions, supporting fair comparison and better understanding of insurance offerings. Consumer protection also emphasizes the importance of the claims process, requiring claims to be handled promptly and fairly. Regulations ensure that insurers process claims within designated timeframes, provide explanations for denials, and offer the right to appeal, which prevents unnecessary delays and ensures that consumers receive due benefits. Additionally, measures against unfair trade practices like post-claim underwriting and misrepresentation protect consumers from exploitative behaviors, with penalties for violations ranging from fines to license revocation.

Beyond regulatory enforcement, consumer protection involves educating policyholders about their rights and providing resources to help them navigate the complexities of insurance. Many state insurance departments offer counseling services and educational materials, and advocacy groups actively push for policies that enhance consumer rights. Furthermore, established mechanisms allow consumers to lodge complaints against insurers, with state regulators mediating to resolve disputes and identify industry-wide issues that may require systemic changes.

The impact of robust consumer protection is profound, enhancing consumer confidence and fostering a competitive market environment where insurers prioritize improving customer service and product offerings. This encourages industry innovation and efficiency and leads to the development of insurance products that more effectively meet consumer needs. In sum, consumer protection is foundational to the integrity and sustainability of the insurance industry, ensuring that the sector remains reliable, accountable, and responsive to the needs of its clientele.

Unfair trade practices in the insurance industry encompass a range of unethical behaviors and actions that undermine the fairness and integrity of insurance transactions. These practices can significantly harm consumers, distort the competitive market environment, and erode trust in the insurance sector as a whole. Addressing unfair trade practices is crucial for regulators and the industry to ensure that consumers are treated equitably and that the market operates efficiently.

Definition and Examples of Unfair Trade Practices

Unfair trade practices in insurance include any deceptive, misleading, or unethical conduct that may misguide a consumer during an insurance policy's purchase, sale, or management. Common examples include:

- **Misrepresentation and False Advertising:** Providing incorrect or misleading information about what an insurance policy covers or the terms of coverage.

- **Twisting:** Persuading a policyholder to cancel, lapse, or switch policies unnecessarily to generate commissions.

- **Sliding:** Adding additional coverage or products without the policyholder's explicit consent or misleading them about the necessity of the added features.

- **Redlining:** Refusing to insure, renew, or offer coverage at reasonable rates based solely on geographic locations without actuarial justification.

- **Claim Denial and Delay Tactics:** Deliberately using tactics to avoid paying claims, such as by misinterpreting policy language or requiring unnecessary documentation.

Regulatory Framework and Enforcement

To combat unfair trade practices, regulatory frameworks at both state and federal levels provide guidelines and statutes that outline prohibited behaviors. State insurance commissioners have significant roles in monitoring insurance activities and enforcing laws that protect consumers from unfair practices. Enforcement actions can include fines, restitution orders for consumers, and, in severe cases, revoking an insurer's license to operate.

Insurance regulators also conduct regular market conduct examinations and audits to assess insurer practices and ensure compliance with regulatory standards. These proactive measures help identify potential areas of concern before they result in widespread consumer harm.

Impact of Unfair Trade Practices on Consumers

Unfair trade practices can have devastating financial and emotional impacts on consumers. For instance, when insurers unjustly deny claims, policyholders may be left with significant out-of-pocket expenses for medical treatments or repairs that they believed were covered under their policies. Moreover, practices such as twisting or sliding can lead to consumers purchasing inappropriate or costly insurance products that do not meet their needs, potentially leading to financial strain.

Preventive Measures and Consumer Education

To prevent unfair trade practices, ongoing consumer education plays a vital role. By informing consumers about their rights and what constitutes unfair practices, regulatory bodies and consumer advocacy groups can empower individuals to make informed decisions and recognize when they may be subjected to unethical behavior.

Insurance companies are also responsible for thoroughly training their agents and representatives on ethical standards and legal requirements. Internal controls and regular training can ensure that all employees understand the importance of fair consumer treatment and the consequences of violating trust.

Collaboration for Improvement

Addressing unfair trade practices requires collaboration among regulators, insurance companies, consumer advocacy groups, and policyholders. Effective communication and information sharing can lead to better detection of unethical practices and more robust preventive measures.

The fight against unfair trade practices is ongoing and vital for maintaining consumer confidence and ensuring a healthy insurance marketplace. Through stringent regulatory oversight, consumer education, and ethical business practices, the insurance industry can strive to eliminate unfair trade practices and uphold its commitment to fair and equitable service to all policyholders.

FRAUD AND ABUSE

Insurance fraud and abuse are pervasive issues that significantly impact the insurance industry, leading to higher premiums for all policyholders and undermining the integrity of the insurance system. Insurance fraud can be committed by applicants, policyholders, third parties, and professionals within the industry, and it ranges from exaggerated claims to intentionally causing an event that can trigger a claim. Recognizing, preventing, and addressing these acts are critical tasks for insurers and regulatory bodies alike.

Types of Insurance Fraud

Insurance fraud is broadly categorized into two types: hard fraud and soft fraud.

- **Hard Fraud:** This involves deliberately faking an accident, injury, theft, arson, or other losses to receive payment from an insurance company. Hard fraud is premeditated and often involves sophisticated schemes and criminal networks.

- **Soft Fraud:** Also known as opportunistic fraud, this occurs when a policyholder or claimant exaggerates a legitimate claim. For example, adding extra items to a list of stolen goods after a burglary or overstating the damages or injuries incurred in an accident.

Beyond these, there are specific types of fraud prevalent in different lines of insurance:

- **Auto Insurance Fraud:** Staging car accidents, reporting higher repair costs, or faking thefts.

- **Health Insurance Fraud:** Billing for services not rendered, upcoding services and equipment, and performing unnecessary procedures to increase insurance payments.

- **Life Insurance Fraud:** Faking death or disability, or omitting information during the application process.

- **Property Insurance Fraud:** Overestimating the value of claimed items or fabricating events that lead to property damage.

Impact of Fraud on the Industry

The economic impact of insurance fraud is staggering. According to estimates by the FBI, the total cost of insurance fraud (excluding health insurance) is more than $40 billion per year. Policyholders ultimately bear this cost through increased premiums—approximately $400 to $700 in additional premiums each year per family.

Detecting and Preventing Fraud

Insurers employ a variety of strategies to detect and prevent fraud:

- **Data Analytics and Technology:** Advanced analytical tools help identify patterns that might indicate fraudulent activity. Machine learning models can detect anomalies in claims or behavior that deviate from the norm.

- **Investigations:** Insurance companies often have special investigative units (SIUs) that review claims suspected of being fraudulent. These units use various investigative techniques, including surveillance, interviews, and review of claims history.

- **Education and Training:** Educating employees and consumers about the indicators of fraud and the importance of reporting suspicious activities is crucial. Many insurers conduct regular training sessions for their staff on anti-fraud measures.

Regulatory and Legal Framework

In the United States, both federal and state laws address insurance fraud. At the state level, all states have laws that make committing insurance fraud a crime, and many have specific anti-fraud mandates that require insurers to set up programs to combat fraud actively. At the federal level, the Department of Justice handles cases of insurance fraud that violate federal laws or involve interstate commerce.

Licensing requirements in the insurance industry are crucial for maintaining the professionalism and integrity of those who sell and manage insurance policies. These requirements ensure that insurance professionals have the necessary knowledge, skills, and ethical understanding to provide accurate and reliable information to consumers.

Purpose of Licensing

Licensing serves several essential functions:

- **Ensuring Competency:** Licensing exams and requirements ensure that insurance professionals are competent in their field and fully understand the products they are selling, including the benefits, limitations, and costs of those products.

- **Promoting Ethics:** Ethical standards are fundamental to the licensing requirements, aiming to foster trust between consumers and insurance professionals. These standards help prevent abuses such as misrepresentation of products or conflicts of interest.

- **Consumer Protection:** By requiring insurance agents and brokers to be licensed, regulators help protect consumers from fraudulent and unethical practices. Licensing provides a mechanism through which consumers can verify the credentials of an insurance professional and file complaints if necessary.

Licensing Process

The licensing process for insurance agents and brokers typically involves several steps:

- **Pre-Licensing Education:** Most states require candidates to complete a certain number of hours of professional education before sitting for the licensing exam. This education covers a broad range of topics relevant to insurance, including state laws and regulations.

- **Licensing Examination:** The examination tests a candidate's knowledge of insurance concepts, state laws governing insurance, and ethical standards. Exams are specific to different lines of insurance, such as life, health, property, and casualty.

- **Application and Background Checks:** After passing the examination, candidates must apply for a license with their state's insurance department, which often includes a background check to identify any criminal history or previous issues with professional licenses.

- **Continuing Education:** Insurance professionals must complete continuing education courses periodically to maintain their licenses. These requirements are intended to keep agents and brokers up-to-date with insurance laws, products, and practice changes.

Challenges and Considerations

One of the challenges in licensing is ensuring consistency and reciprocity between states. While most states have similar basic requirements, specific rules and continuing education requirements can vary significantly. This can create barriers for professionals who operate in multiple states. To address this, some states participate in reciprocity agreements that recognize each other's licenses, facilitating easier cross-state business operations.

The robust regulatory framework governing licensing and the comprehensive strategies to combat insurance fraud collectively uphold the insurance industry's standards, ensuring that it operates efficiently, ethically, and to the benefit of all stakeholders involved.

Continuing Education

Continuing Education (CE) is integral to the professional development of insurance agents and brokers. Mandated by state insurance departments, CE is designed to ensure that insurance professionals remain knowledgeable about current laws, regulations, new insurance products, and the ever-evolving dynamics of the insurance industry. This requirement not only reinforces the expertise necessary to serve clients effectively but also upholds the integrity and credibility of the insurance profession.

Purpose of Continuing Education

The primary goal of continuing education in insurance is to maintain a high standard of professional practice. It helps insurance agents stay informed about changes in the insurance landscape, including updates in laws and regulations, innovations in insurance products and services, and advancements in related technology. By continuously updating their knowledge base, insurance professionals can provide better advice to clients, enhancing consumer protection and trust in the industry.

CE Requirements

Continuing education requirements vary significantly between states but generally involve a specific number of hours licensed insurance professionals must complete within a given renewal period, usually every one or two years. State-approved educational institutions often provide these courses, and can be achieved through in-person classes, online courses, or seminars. The content of CE courses is carefully selected to cover relevant topics beneficial for insurance professionals. Typical subjects include ethical practices in insurance, updates on state and federal insurance laws, specific information on lines of insurance such as life, health, property, and casualty, and courses on risk management, claims handling, and customer service.

Impact of CE on Professional Practice

Continuing education plays a critical role in enhancing the professional skills of insurance agents. It ensures that they are competent in their field and capable of adapting to new regulations and market conditions. This adaptability is crucial in a landscape as complex and regulated as insurance, where professionals must navigate a myriad of rules that can have significant implications for their business operations and the advice they provide to clients.

Furthermore, CE helps to foster a culture of lifelong learning within the industry, encouraging professionals to pursue further knowledge and specialization. This dedication to ongoing education can lead to better career opportunities, higher professional standards, and increased respect from clients and peers.

While continuing education is fundamentally beneficial, it can present challenges such as finding the time to complete courses amidst a busy work schedule, the financial cost of education, and ensuring the courses' relevance. However, the digital age has brought significant improvements in how CE is delivered. Online platforms now provide flexible and accessible learning options, making it easier for professionals to fulfill their CE requirements.

Additionally, there is a growing recognition of the need for more tailored and advanced educational offerings to keep pace with the rapid changes in the industry, such as cybersecurity in insurance and the implications of emerging technologies like blockchain and artificial intelligence. This evolution in CE content enriches the knowledge of seasoned professionals and ensures that new entrants to the field are well-prepared to handle modern challenges.

ADVERTISING GUIDELINES

Advertising plays a pivotal role in insurance companies' marketing strategies, helping them reach new clients and communicate the benefits of their products. However, due to the complexity and importance of insurance services, some stringent guidelines and regulations govern how insurance is advertised to ensure that consumers are not misled.

Regulatory Framework for Insurance Advertising

Insurance advertising is heavily regulated to protect consumers from deceptive or misleading information that could influence their decision-making. Regulatory bodies at both state and federal levels have established comprehensive guidelines that dictate what is permissible in insurance advertising. These regulations ensure that all advertising materials are truthful, not misleading, and clearly present the insurance products' details.

The guidelines typically require that all advertisements identify the insurance company's name and the specific insurance product being offered. Ads must not use terms or phrases that could mislead a consumer about the nature of the policy, the benefits it provides, or the terms of coverage. Additionally, advertisements must not create false impressions regarding a policy's cost or benefits.

Ethical Considerations in Advertising

Ethics in advertising is another crucial aspect underpinning consumer trust and confidence in the insurance industry. Insurance companies must avoid practices such as using fear-based tactics or making ambiguous promises that could mislead consumers. The ethical responsibility extends to ensuring that all demographic groups are represented fairly in advertising materials and that the marketing strategies do not discriminate against or exclude any potential clients.

Monitoring and Compliance

State insurance departments and other regulatory agencies monitor compliance with advertising guidelines. These bodies have the authority to review advertising materials, demand corrections, and impose penalties for violations, including fines, cease-and-desist orders, and, in severe cases, the revocation of licenses to sell insurance.

Insurance companies often have dedicated compliance teams to ensure that all advertising materials meet regulatory standards before they are published or broadcast. This internal oversight is crucial in maintaining compliance and protecting the company from potential legal and reputational risks.

Impact of Effective Advertising

Effective advertising can greatly benefit the insurance industry when done within the bounds of regulatory and ethical guidelines. It can educate consumers about available insurance options, promote better understanding of complex products, and enhance the overall marketability of insurance offerings. Well-crafted advertising campaigns can demystify insurance products, making them more accessible and appealing to a broader audience, thereby expanding market reach and driving business growth.

Continuing education and adherence to advertising guidelines are foundational to maintaining the insurance industry's professionalism, integrity, and efficiency. These elements ensure that insurance professionals remain knowledgeable and ethical in their practices, ultimately fostering a healthier marketplace and a better-informed consumer base.

COMPLAINT PROCEDURES

Complaint procedures within the insurance industry are a critical component of consumer protection. They provide a formal mechanism for policyholders and consumers to voice their concerns and seek resolution when they feel their rights have been violated or are dissatisfied with the services received. Effective complaint procedures ensure that consumers can report problems and serve as a vital feedback loop for insurers and regulatory bodies, helping them improve practices and prevent future issues. This section delves into the importance of these procedures, the steps involved in filing a complaint, and the impact on the insurance industry.

Importance of Complaint Procedures

The primary importance of complaint procedures lies in their role in upholding consumer rights and fostering transparency within the insurance industry. When consumers know that they have a reliable avenue to address their grievances, it enhances their trust in the insurance system. These procedures ensure that insurers adhere to legal and ethical standards and provide recourse for policyholders affected by potential mismanagement or misconduct.

Steps in the Complaint Process

1. **Internal Review by the Insurance Company:** Most insurers encourage policyholders to first address their complaints directly with the company before seeking external mediation. Insurers typically have their own customer service or complaint departments tasked with resolving issues, ranging from misunderstandings regarding policy terms to disputes over claim settlements.

2. **Filing a Formal Complaint:** If the issue is not resolved internally to the consumer's satisfaction, the next step is to file a formal complaint with the state insurance department. This involves submitting a detailed account of the issue, including any supporting documentation, such as correspondence with the insurer, policy documents, and other evidence supporting the complaint.

3. **Investigation by the State Insurance Department:** Upon receiving a complaint, the state insurance department reviews the submission to determine its validity and then proceeds with an investigation. This investigation may involve requesting additional information from both the complainant and the insurer, conducting interviews, and reviewing company practices relevant to the complaint.

4. **Resolution and Enforcement:** After completing the investigation, the state insurance department will issue a decision, which might include ordering the insurer to take corrective action or compensating the complainant. Suppose the insurer is found to be in violation of insurance regulations. In that case, the department may also impose penalties, including fines or other disciplinary actions.

Role of the National Association of Insurance Commissioners (NAIC)

The NAIC plays a significant role in standardizing complaint procedures across states and provides a centralized database where consumers can track complaints and review the complaint histories of insurance companies. This national oversight helps ensure that complaint procedures are uniformly rigorous and effective across different jurisdictions.

Despite the established procedures, managing complaints can be challenging for both insurers and regulatory bodies. Issues such as the complexity of insurance contracts, subjective interpretations of policy language, and the high volume of complaints can complicate the resolution process. Additionally, the emotional and financial stakes for consumers can heighten tensions and increase the pressure on all parties to resolve disputes swiftly.

Impact of Effective Complaint Procedures

Effective complaint procedures have a profound impact on the insurance industry. They promote higher standards of accountability and transparency, which in turn can lead to improved customer satisfaction. A good track record in handling complaints can be a significant competitive advantage for insurers, enhancing their reputation and trustworthiness in the market.

Moreover, the feedback garnered from complaint procedures provides valuable insights into common areas of dissatisfaction, which can guide industry practices and regulatory changes. By addressing these systemic issues, insurers and regulators can reduce the incidence of disputes and enhance the overall quality of service. Complaint procedures are an essential aspect of the regulatory framework in the insurance industry. They protect consumer interests, enhance industry standards, and contribute to the overall stability and credibility of the insurance market. By ensuring that these procedures are robust, accessible, and effectively managed, regulators and insurers can significantly improve how consumer grievances are addressed and resolved, ultimately benefiting the entire insurance ecosystem.

CHAPTER 5

PREPARING FOR THE EXAM

Welcome to Chapter 5! As we approach the culmination of our journey through the intricacies of insurance knowledge, this chapter is dedicated to equipping you with the tools and strategies necessary for effective exam preparation. Having explored the broad landscape of insurance regulations and products, it's now time to focus on how best to consolidate and apply this wealth of information in an exam environment.

Preparing for an exam, especially as crucial as the Life and Health Insurance Licensing Examination, isn't just about memorizing facts and figures; it's about understanding concepts in depth and recalling and applying them under exam conditions. This chapter will look at proven study techniques, time management tips, common exam mistakes to avoid, and strategies to overcome exam anxiety. Our aim is to prepare you for success on exam day and develop skills that will serve you throughout your insurance career.

Let us embark on this final leg of our preparation journey confidently and determinedly. In Chapter 5, we will lay the foundation for your successful transition from student to licensed insurance professional. Are you ready? Let's dive into our first topic: Study Techniques.

STUDY TECHNIQUES

Preparing for the Life and Health Insurance License Exam requires a strong grasp of insurance concepts and regulations and the deployment of effective study techniques. These techniques can significantly enhance one's ability to absorb, retain, and recall information, thereby improving performance on the exam. Effective study strategies are not merely about reviewing material but engaging with it in a manner that promotes deeper understanding and long-term retention.

Active Learning

Active learning is a cornerstone of effective studying, especially for an exam as detailed and expansive as the insurance license exam. This approach involves dynamically interacting with the material rather than passively reading or listening. Techniques under this umbrella include:

- **Teaching the Material:** One of the most effective ways to understand a topic is to explain it to someone else. This not only clarifies your own understanding but also highlights areas where your knowledge may be lacking.

- **Applying Concepts to Real-World Scenarios:** Using hypothetical scenarios to apply insurance principles can help solidify complex concepts and regulations, making them more memorable and easier to recall during the exam.

Distributed Practice

Spacing out study sessions over some time (distributed practice) is far more effective than cramming all study into one long session (massed practice). This technique helps by:

- **Enhancing Retention:** Regular review of material over weeks or months leads to better retention of information than the same amount of study crammed in a single session.

- **Building Understanding Gradually:** Complex regulations and policies can be broken down into manageable sections and learned incrementally.

Multimodal Learning

Different people prefer different learning styles—visual, auditory, reading/writing, and kinesthetic. Employing multiple senses to study can enhance understanding and retention:

- **Visual Learning:** Charts, graphs, and diagrams can help visualize information, making it easier to remember.

- **Auditory Learning:** Listening to recorded lectures or discussing topics with peers can reinforce auditory learners' comprehension.

- **Kinesthetic Learning:** Engaging in activities like role-playing different insurance scenarios can help kinesthetic learners grasp concepts more effectively.

Utilization of Study Aids

Several study aids can bolster understanding and retention:

- **Flashcards:** These are excellent for memorizing definitions, policies, and regulations. They can be used for quick review sessions, especially during short breaks throughout the day.

- **Mind Maps:** Creating mind maps can help connect different concepts in a visual network, making it easier to see how various insurance rules and products interrelate.

- **Study Guides and Prep Books:** Comprehensive study guides and prep books tailored specifically for the insurance exams can provide structured learning and highlight key areas to focus on.

Practice Testing

Taking regular practice tests is perhaps one of the most vital study techniques:

- **Familiarity with Exam Format:** Practice tests help students become familiar with the format and types of questions that will be on the actual exam.

- **Identification of Weak Areas:** Regular testing makes it clear which areas need more attention, allowing students to focus subsequent study sessions more effectively.

- **Reducing Exam Anxiety:** By simulating the exam experience, practice tests reduce anxiety and increase confidence.

Feedback and Adjustment

It's important to assess periodically how well your study techniques are working. This might involve:

- **Seeking Feedback:** Discussing complex topics with peers or mentors can provide new insights and enhance understanding.

- **Adjusting Strategies:** Based on performance in practice tests and overall comfort with the material, students may need to adjust their study strategies, dedicating more time to weaker areas or changing their study methods.

In conclusion, preparing effectively for the Life and Health Insurance License Exam involves a strategic approach to learning. By employing a variety of study techniques tailored to one's personal learning style and making adjustments based on feedback, prospective insurance agents can significantly enhance their likelihood of passing the exam and advancing their careers.

TIME MANAGEMENT

Time management is crucial for effectively preparing for the Life and Health Insurance License Exam. Mastering this skill ensures that you cover all necessary material thoroughly without the added stress of cramming information at the last minute. It involves planning your study schedule, setting priorities, and maintaining a disciplined approach to your learning process. Well-organized time management enhances your ability to absorb and retain information and significantly reduces exam-related anxiety.

Developing a Study Plan

Creating a detailed study plan is the first step in effective time management. This plan should outline what topics need to be covered and allocate specific times for studying each section. Break down the content into manageable segments that can be learned throughout your preparation. This helps create a balanced approach, preventing any topic from overwhelming your study sessions.

1. **Set Realistic Goals**: Start by setting achievable goals for each study session. Determine how much time you can dedicate daily or weekly towards exam preparation, taking into account your personal and professional obligations.

2. **Prioritize Content**: Prioritize topics based on their complexity and importance on the exam. Focus more time on areas where you feel less confident and on topics that carry more weight in the exam structure.

3. **Schedule Reviews**: Regular review sessions are essential to reinforce your memory and understanding of the material. Schedule weekly and monthly reviews to review previously studied content, which helps long-term retention.

Effective Use of Time

Effective use of time is not just about studying hard but studying smart. This involves identifying the best times of the day when you are most alert and productive to conduct your study sessions.

1. **Active Study Sessions**: Engage in active studying methods like summarizing notes, creating mind maps, or discussing topics with peers. These methods are more productive than passive reading and help in deeper comprehension.

2. **Avoid Multitasking**: Focus on one topic at a time to ensure that you fully understand the material before moving on to the next. Multitasking can reduce the quality of your learning and lead to information overload.

3. **Take Breaks**: Short breaks between study sessions can help maintain your concentration levels and prevent burnout. Techniques such as the Pomodoro Technique, where you study intensely for short periods followed by a break, can be very effective.

Monitoring Progress

It's essential to monitor your progress as you prepare for the exam. This helps adjust your study plan according to your needs and motivates you by providing a sense of accomplishment.

1. **Checklists and Timelines**: Use checklists to mark topics you have covered. Set timelines for reaching certain milestones in your study plan.

2. **Practice Tests**: Regularly taking practice tests can help track your readiness for the exam. It also assists in identifying areas that need more focus, allowing you to adjust your study plan accordingly.

Balancing Study and Personal Time

Finally, while preparing for the exam is essential, balancing your study time with personal time is crucial. Ensure you maintain a healthy work-life-study balance to keep stress levels manageable and your outlook positive.

In conclusion, effective time management is about creating a structured and balanced study plan that allows for comprehensive coverage of the exam material, regular reviews, and personal downtime. By following these strategies, you can maximize your productivity, enhance learning outcomes, and approach your exam day confidently and calmly.

COMMON EXAM MISTAKES

Preparing for the Life and Health Insurance License Exam is a meticulous process that involves understanding complex concepts and navigating the potential pitfalls that can hinder performance. Awareness of common exam mistakes is crucial as it helps candidates steer clear of errors that might compromise their success. This section explores some typical errors exam takers make and offers insights into how to avoid them.

One frequent mistake is poor time management during the exam itself. Candidates often spend too much time on difficult questions, leaving insufficient time to address the remaining ones adequately. A more effective approach is to initially skip questions that seem too complex and return to them after completing the easier ones. This strategy ensures that all questions receive attention and that those likely to be answered correctly are not missed due to time constraints.

Another standard error is failing to read exam questions thoroughly. In the rush to answer as many questions as possible, candidates sometimes skim through questions too quickly, missing crucial details or misinterpreting what is being asked. Slowing down to carefully read and consider each question can prevent this oversight. It's essential to look out for keywords and be mindful of absolutes such as "always" or "never," which can change the meaning of a question entirely.

Over-reliance on memorized answers without understanding the underlying principles is also a pitfall. The insurance exam tests comprehension of concepts, not just the ability to recall facts. Candidates should focus on grasping the principles behind the rules and regulations of insurance practices. This deeper understanding will enable them to tackle application-based questions more effectively, rather than just those requiring memorized information recollection.

Mismanagement of exam preparation time often leads to an uneven grasp of the necessary material. Candidates sometimes concentrate their study efforts disproportionately on certain topics they feel comfortable with or deem important, neglecting others that are equally crucial. This can result in a lopsided preparation where some parts of the exam content are well understood while others are barely covered. A balanced study plan that allocates appropriate time to all topics is essential for a comprehensive understanding and preparedness.

Failing to simulate the exam environment during practice sessions is another oversight. Taking practice exams under conditions that mimic the actual exam setting can help candidates adapt to the pressure and format of the real test. This includes timing the practice sessions, using the same sitting durations, and following the same rules as the actual exam. Such simulations help build stamina and focus, reducing anxiety on exam day.

Additionally, many candidates neglect the importance of rest and good physical health as part of their exam preparation. Cramming late into the night before the exam can diminish cognitive function and focus. Ensuring adequate rest, maintaining a healthy diet, and engaging in moderate exercise in the days leading up to the exam can significantly boost mental alertness and stamina.

By being mindful of these common mistakes and actively working to avoid them, candidates can significantly enhance their performance on the insurance license exam. This proactive approach prepares them to tackle the exam confidently and instills habits that contribute to long-term success in their insurance careers.

MEMORIZATION TIPS

Effective memorization is a critical skill for those preparing for the Life and Health Insurance License Exam. Given the extensive amount of information that candidates need to recall, developing strong memorization techniques can significantly enhance one's ability to retain and retrieve key concepts and details during the exam. Here are some strategies that can help streamline the memorization process.

Firstly, using mnemonics is an incredibly powerful tool for memorization. Mnemonics are memory aids that help organize and recall information more easily. For example, using acronyms or making up rhymes can make remembering complex insurance regulations or lists of principles more manageable. These techniques transform hard-to-remember details into something simpler and more relatable, which enhances the ability to recall them under exam conditions.

Another effective memorization strategy is the loci method, often called the memory palace technique. This method involves visualizing a familiar place and associating elements of that space with pieces of information. For instance, imagining walking through your house and assigning different insurance concepts to particular rooms or objects can help anchor this information in your memory. This technique leverages spatial memory which is generally strong in most individuals and can be especially useful for visual learners.

Repetition also plays a crucial role in memorization. Regularly reviewing key concepts and details is essential to move information from short-term to long-term memory. This can involve re-reading textbook chapters, rewriting notes, or repeatedly testing oneself with flashcards. Each review session reinforces the neural pathways associated with the specific information, making recall easier and more automatic.

Furthermore, teaching the material to someone else is an excellent way to deepen one's grasp and memorization of the content. Explaining complex insurance policies or regulations to a peer or even to oneself aloud can uncover any gaps in understanding and solidify memory. This active engagement with the material makes the information more likely to be retained.

Organizing information into chunks is another beneficial technique. The human mind can typically hold about seven items in short-term memory at one time. By breaking down information into smaller, logically grouped chunks, you can work within these cognitive limits. For example, grouping insurance concepts by themes such as policy types, underwriting processes, or claim procedures can help manage the volume of information more effectively.

Visualization is yet another helpful memorization technique. Creating vivid mental images for the information you need to remember can make abstract or dry material much more memorable. Associating a complex legal principle with a striking visual metaphor or symbol can help lock it into your memory.

Finally, integrating physical activity into study sessions can boost memorization. Studies suggest that mild physical exercise, such as walking, can enhance cognitive function and memory due to the increased blood flow and oxygen to the brain. Even short walks during study breaks can be beneficial.

By employing these memorization strategies, candidates can enhance their ability to recall a broad range of information quickly and accurately, thus improving their performance on the Life and Health Insurance License Exam. These techniques aid in exam preparation and professional practices where quick recall of extensive information is often required.

PRACTICE EXAM

Incorporating practice exams into the preparation process for the Life and Health Insurance License Exam is indispensable for several reasons. Practice tests provide a benchmark for a candidate's understanding and readiness and expose the examinee to the format and types of questions they will encounter, reducing surprises and increasing confidence on exam day.

Simulating the Exam Environment

Practice exams are most effective when they simulate the actual exam environment. This means adhering to the specific time limits, completing the practice test in a quiet environment, and using only the materials that will be allowed during the real exam. This level of simulation helps candidates manage their time effectively, understand the pressure of working under exam conditions, and build stamina for the mental endurance required on test day.

Identifying Strengths and Weaknesses

One of the primary benefits of practice exams is that they allow candidates to identify areas of strength and weakness in their knowledge. This is crucial for efficient study planning. By analyzing performance on practice exams, candidates can pinpoint which topics need more attention and which they have mastered. This targeted approach ensures that study time is not wasted on reviewing material that is already well understood; instead, it is focused on areas that will most improve overall exam performance.

Familiarity with Question Formats

Insurance exams can include various question types, from multiple-choice to true/false and scenario-based questions. Practice exams help candidates become familiar with these formats, reducing the cognitive load involved in understanding how to answer different types of questions during the actual exam. This familiarity allows candidates to focus solely on the content of the questions rather than figuring out how to approach them.

Reducing Test Anxiety

Test anxiety is a common issue for many examinees and can significantly impact performance. Regularly taking practice exams helps mitigate this anxiety by familiarizing candidates with the testing process. As the exam approaches, practice tests transform from daunting challenges into familiar tasks. This familiarity breeds confidence, which is crucial for reducing anxiety and improving performance.

Application of Knowledge

Practice exams also allow candidates to apply theoretical knowledge in a practical context. Many insurance concepts and policies can be abstract and complex. Practice exams require candidates to use this knowledge in ways that mirror how they will need to apply it in real-world scenarios as professionals. This application reinforces learning and deepens understanding, making knowledge more likely to be retained long-term.

Feedback and Adjustment

Finally, practice exams provide immediate feedback. This feedback is essential for making adjustments to study plans and strategies. Suppose a candidate consistently makes errors in a particular question or topic. This signals a need for further review or a different approach to studying that material. Additionally, reviewing incorrect answers helps consolidate learning by correcting misunderstandings and reinforcing the correct information.

TEST ANXIETY

Test anxiety is a common challenge faced by many candidates preparing for the Life and Health Insurance License Exam. It can manifest as nervousness, worry, or fear, significantly impacting one's ability to perform well during the test. Understanding how to manage and mitigate test anxiety is crucial for exam takers to ensure they can demonstrate their knowledge effectively under exam conditions.

Understanding Test Anxiety

Test anxiety often stems from fear of failure, pressure to perform, or negative past experiences with testing. Symptoms can range from mild nervousness to severe anxiety, including physical symptoms like sweating, rapid heartbeat, and nausea, as well as psychological symptoms such as difficulty concentrating, blanking out, or negative thinking patterns.

Strategies to Overcome Test Anxiety

1. **Preparation and Practice:** Adequate preparation is the most effective way to reduce test anxiety. Thorough understanding and mastery of the exam material through consistent study and practice can boost confidence. Practice exams are particularly beneficial as they help familiarize candidates with the format and timing of the actual test, reducing fear of the unknown.

2. **Mindfulness and Relaxation Techniques:** Techniques such as deep breathing, meditation, and progressive muscle relaxation can be very effective in managing physical and mental symptoms of anxiety. Regular practice of these techniques leading up to the exam day can help maintain calm and focus during the test.

3. **Positive Visualization:** Visualization techniques involve picturing oneself succeeding and performing well during the exam. This mental rehearsal can enhance self-confidence and reduce anxiety by mentally preparing the candidate for a positive outcome.

4. **Cognitive Restructuring** involves identifying and challenging negative thoughts about the exam or one's abilities and replacing them with more positive and realistic thoughts. Understanding that it is normal to feel some anxiety and acknowledging that it can be a sign of preparedness rather than a predictor of failure can also help reshape one's perspective on the anxiety experienced.

5. **Healthy Physical Habits:** Good physical health can influence mental state. Adequate sleep, nutritious food, and regular physical exercise can improve overall anxiety management. Avoiding excessive caffeine and sugar before the exam can also prevent spikes in anxiety.

6. **Seeking Professional Help:** For some, test anxiety can be overwhelming and difficult to manage alone. In such cases, it might be beneficial to consult with a counselor or psychologist who can provide professional strategies and support to cope with anxiety.

Implementing the Strategies

On the exam day, arriving early and having a routine to settle into the testing environment calmly is essential. Having a simple pre-test routine, such as deep breathing exercises or reviewing concise notes, can set a positive tone for the session.

Understanding and implementing these strategies can significantly alleviate the effects of test anxiety, enabling candidates to approach the Life and Health Insurance License Exam with confidence and clarity. By addressing anxiety proactively, candidates can ensure that it does not hinder their ability to pass the exam and move forward in their professional careers.

EXAM DAY STRATEGIES

Exam day can be pivotal for candidates aspiring to succeed in the Life and Health Insurance License Exam. Implementing effective strategies on this day is crucial to maximizing performance and ensuring all the hard work and preparation pay off. Here are some essential tactics to employ on exam day:

1. Morning Preparation: Start the day with a nutritious breakfast that balances protein, fats, and carbohydrates to maintain energy levels throughout the exam. Avoid high-sugar foods that can lead to an energy crash. Ensure that you gather and pack all necessary materials the night before, including identification, admission ticket, approved calculators, and other allowed resources.

2. Arrival at the Testing Center: Plan to arrive at the testing center early to avoid any last-minute stress and to allow time for check-in procedures. Familiarize yourself with the testing environment if possible. This can help reduce anxiety and provide comfort with the surroundings.

3. Time Management During the Exam: Prioritize time management once the exam starts. Scan through the entire exam to gauge the question types and difficulty levels. Tackle easier questions first to secure quick points and build confidence, leaving more time for complex problems. Keep track of time, allotting it in a way that all questions are at least reviewed, if not thoroughly answered.

4. Reading Questions Carefully: Take the time to read each question carefully to avoid common pitfalls such as misreading or overlooking critical details. Pay attention to keywords and be wary of absolutes like "always" or "never," which can often indicate incorrect answers.

5. Managing Stress and Maintaining Focus: If you become anxious or lose focus, take brief moments to practice deep breathing or other quick relaxation techniques. This can help reset your focus and reduce anxiety, allowing you to maintain efficiency throughout the exam.

POST-EXAM REVIEW

Once the exam is over, the learning and development process should continue, especially in anticipation of future professional requirements or potential reexamination:

1. Initial Reflection: After completing the exam, reflect on the experience while it is still fresh in your mind. Note any areas that were particularly challenging or questions that were unexpected. This can be invaluable for future preparation if you need to retake the exam or help guide others.

2. Review of Exam Performance: When scores are released, thoroughly review your performance. Most exams will provide some insight into areas of strength and weakness. Analyze areas where you scored lower than expected and consider revisiting these topics as part of your continuing education.

3. Learning from the Experience: Regardless of the outcome, each exam experience is a learning opportunity. Whether you pass or need to retake the exam, consider what worked well and what could be improved in your study and exam-taking strategies. Use this analysis to adjust future learning and preparation methods.

4. Continuing Education Planning: After passing the exam, start planning your continuing education. The insurance industry is constantly evolving, and staying updated through continued learning is crucial. Identify courses, workshops, or seminars that align with your career goals and areas of interest. This will fulfill mandatory continuing education requirements and enhance your professional growth and competency in your field.

Implementing these strategies for exam day and beyond not only sets the foundation for a successful exam performance but also for ongoing professional development and success in the insurance industry. These efforts ensure that candidates are well-prepared not just for the exam but for a thriving career in insurance

CONTINUING EDUCATION PLANNING

After successfully navigating the Life and Health Insurance License Exam, it is important to not view this achievement as the final step in your professional development. In the dynamic field of insurance, continuing education (CE) is crucial for maintaining competence, compliance, and competitive edge in the industry. This section outlines strategies for effective continuing education planning, ensuring that insurance professionals remain knowledgeable about evolving industry practices, legislation, and market trends.

Importance of Continuing Education

Continuing education serves multiple purposes in the insurance industry. It ensures that professionals are up-to-date with the latest regulations and practices, helping them to provide the best advice and service to their clients. CE is also often legally required to maintain licensure in many states, underlining its importance from a compliance perspective.

Strategic Planning for Continuing Education

1. **Assessment of Educational Needs:** Start by assessing your professional needs and interests. Identify areas where the industry is changing, such as digital advancements, regulatory updates, or shifts in consumer behavior. Also, consider areas where your knowledge could be deeper, which will enhance your ability to serve your clients better.

2. **Setting Goals:** Set specific, measurable, achievable, relevant, and time-bound (SMART) goals for your continuing education. These goals might relate to mastering certain areas of your practice, learning new skills, or achieving higher certifications. Having clear objectives can guide your choices in CE courses and keep you motivated.

3. **Choosing the Right Courses:** Select courses that align with your set goals and fulfill any state-specific licensing requirements. Look for accredited programs that offer up-to-date, comprehensive content and provide practical knowledge that can be directly applied to your work.

4. **Scheduling:** Plan your educational activities throughout the year to avoid last-minute cramming or conflicts with professional responsibilities. Spreading out your learning can help with better absorption of information and less stress.

5. **Leveraging Resources:** Utilize resources offered by professional associations, insurance companies, and continuing education providers. Many organizations offer seminars, webinars, and workshops that count towards CE credits and provide networking opportunities with peers and thought leaders.

Integration into Professional Practice

The knowledge gained from continuing education should be actively integrated into your professional practice. Apply new skills and insights to enhance service delivery, advise clients more effectively, and improve operational efficiencies. Sharing new knowledge with colleagues and clients not only reinforces your own learning but also contributes to your organization's overall professionalism and capability.

Having established a foundation for ongoing professional development, we invite you to move forward to Section 2 of this guide, where you can apply and test your understanding through a series of multiple-choice questions. This next section is designed to reinforce the topics we have covered so far and to simulate real-world application of your knowledge in a structured testing format. Whether you are reviewing key concepts or testing your readiness for re-certification, these practice questions will provide valuable insights into your areas of strength and opportunities for further learning.

As you continue on this journey, remember that each step in your education not only enhances your ability to perform in your role but also elevates the standard of service within the insurance industry as a whole. Let's proceed to Section 2 and continue our path to professional excellence.

SECTION II

MULTIPLE CHOICE QUESTIONS

Chapter 1: Understanding the Fundamentals

1. What is the primary purpose of life insurance?
   A) Investment returns
   B) Provide financial security to dependents
   C) Tax avoidance
   D) Employment benefits

2. Which type of health insurance policy is best suited for covering day-to-day medical expenses?
   A) Term Life Insurance
   B) Whole Life Insurance
   C) Major Medical Insurance
   D) Disability Insurance

3. What principle is most directly involved in spreading the risk of loss among policyholders?
   A) Indemnity
   B) Utmost good faith
   C) Proximate cause
   D) Risk pooling

4. In insurance terms, what does the concept of 'utmost good faith' imply?
   A) Insurers are legally obliged to advise on the best product available.
   B) The insurer and the insured have a mutual obligation to disclose all important facts.
   C) Claims must be settled within a fixed period.
   D) Premiums must be affordable.

5. Which type of insurance is primarily used to replace income?
   A) Property insurance
   B) Life insurance
   C) Health insurance
   D) Casualty insurance

6. Which policy feature directly affects the premium cost of a term life insurance policy?
    A) The term length
    B) Investment component
    C) Cash value accumulation
    D) Conversion options

7. What is the key distinguishing feature of a Whole Life Insurance policy?
    A) Coverage for a specified term
    B) Lifetime coverage
    C) Adjustable premiums
    D) High investment returns

8. Under which condition can a beneficiary expect to receive the death benefit from a life insurance policy?
    A) When the policyholder reaches retirement age
    B) Upon the policyholder's death
    C) When the policy matures
    D) When the policyholder discontinues the premium payment

9. What does the 'insurable interest' requirement in life insurance mean?
    A) The beneficiary must be related by blood to the insured.
    B) The policy owner must expect to benefit financially by the continued life of the insured.
    C) The insured must be employed at the time of policy purchase.
    D) The policy owner must have a good credit score.

10. Which is an example of risk avoidance?
    A) Purchasing health insurance
    B) Installing fire alarms in a home
    C) Choosing not to engage in skydiving
    D) Diversifying investment portfolio

Chapter 2: Types of Insurance Policies

11. What distinguishes Term Life Insurance from Whole Life Insurance?
    A) Investment growth potential
    B) Temporary versus permanent coverage
    C) Focus on medical benefits
    D) Eligibility age for coverage

12. Which type of life insurance allows for flexible premiums and a flexible death benefit?
    A) Term Life Insurance
    B) Whole Life Insurance
    C) Universal Life Insurance
    D) Variable Life Insurance

13. How does Universal Life Insurance primarily invest the policyholder's premiums?
    A) Stocks
    B) Bonds
    C) Mutual funds
    D) A mix of investments chosen by the policyholder

14. Variable Life Insurance offers:
    A) Fixed premiums and fixed death benefits
    B) Investment options that can alter the value of the death benefit and cash value
    C) Guaranteed returns on cash values
    D) None of the above

15. Survivorship Life Insurance is ideally suited for:
    A) Parents with dependent children
    B) High-net-worth individuals planning estate taxes
    C) Young singles without dependents
    D) Individuals without any beneficiaries

16. A policy feature that allows the insured to secure insurance for a spouse or child is called:
    A) Conversion privilege
    B) Accelerated benefits
    C) Waiver of premium
    D) Rider

17. Group Life Insurance is typically offered through:
    A) A family policy
    B) Employer benefit packages
    C) Direct purchase by individuals
    D) Government programs

18. Convertible Term Life Insurance policies allow policyholders to:
    A) Transfer policy ownership
    B) Convert the term policy into a whole or universal life policy without a medical exam
    C) Increase the death benefit based on inflation rates
    D) Reduce premiums based on improved health

19. Which type of insurance might include an automatic premium loan feature?
    A) Term Life Insurance
    B) Whole Life Insurance
    C) Universal Life Insurance
    D) Variable Life Insurance

20. In a Whole Life policy, cash value accumulates:
    A) On a tax-deferred basis
    B) And is accessible through withdrawals and policy loans
    C) Both A and B
    D) None of the above

Chapter 3: Insurance Regulations

21. What is the primary role of state insurance departments?
    A) Issuing insurance policies to individuals
    B) Regulating and overseeing insurance companies within the state
    C) Directly managing the claims process for policyholders
    D) Providing funding for insurance companies

22. What does NAIC stand for and what is its purpose?
    A) National Association of Insurance Companies, a trade organization for insurers
    B) National Association of Insurance Commissioners, an organization that helps set standards and regulations
    C) National Agency of Insurance Compliance, a federal regulatory agency
    D) None of the above

23. How do state-specific regulations most commonly impact insurance practices?
    A) They create uniformity across all states
    B) They may vary significantly from state to state, affecting how insurance is practiced locally
    C) They have little impact compared to federal regulations
    D) They only apply to life insurance

24. What is the purpose of market conduct examinations?
    A) To assess the financial stability of insurance companies
    B) To ensure compliance with insurance regulations through reviews of practices and procedures
    C) To evaluate the customer service provided by insurance agents
    D) All of the above

25. Why is consumer protection critical in the insurance industry?
    A) It ensures all consumers are eligible for insurance
    B) It protects consumers from unfair practices and ensures fair treatment
    C) It sets prices for insurance products
    D) It manages the licensing of all insurance agents

26. What are unfair trade practices in the context of insurance?
    A) Practices that provide too many options to the consumer
    B) Ethical standards that govern international insurance practices
    C) Deceptive, misleading, or fraudulent conduct by those in the insurance industry
    D) Legal actions taken by consumers against insurers

27. What does fraud and abuse regulation aim to prevent in insurance?
    A) Over-regulation of insurance practices
    B) Misuse of insurance funds and deceptive practices
    C) Issuance of too many types of insurance policies
    D) Government intervention in insurance operations

28. How do licensing requirements benefit the insurance industry?
    A) By decreasing competition among agents
    B) By ensuring that insurance professionals are qualified and knowledgeable
    C) By limiting the number of available insurance products
    D) By reducing consumer choice in the market

29. What role do continuing education requirements play in the insurance industry?
    A) They ensure that insurance professionals do not need to renew their licenses
    B) They help maintain high professional standards and up-to-date knowledge
    C) They prevent new insurance companies from entering the market
    D) They are optional and not necessary for maintaining licensure

30. How are complaints against insurance companies typically handled?
    A) Through internal company reviews only

B) By federal government courts
C) Through state insurance department investigations and resolutions
D) They are generally ignored unless they reach a certain quantity

Chapter 4: Preparing for the Exam

31. Which study technique is recommended for understanding complex material deeply?
    A) Skimming through materials quickly before the exam
    B) Focusing solely on memorization of facts
    C) Engaging with the material through teaching or group discussions
    D) Limiting study sessions to once a week

32. What is the most effective way to manage time during the exam?
    A) Answer all questions in order, regardless of difficulty
    B) Spend equal time on every question
    C) Quickly answer easy questions to allow more time for difficult ones
    D) Focus on the hardest questions first to get them out of the way

33. What common mistake should be avoided regarding the use of practice exams?
    A) Taking too many practice exams
    B) Using practice exams to familiarize oneself with the format and timing
    C) Relying on practice exams as the sole form of study
    D) Reviewing incorrect answers on practice exams

34. Why is it important to develop a routine for exam day?
    A) To ensure you arrive at the right location
    B) To minimize anxiety and establish a mental readiness for the exam
    C) To meet other exam candidates
    D) To learn last-minute material

35. How can candidates mitigate test anxiety effectively?
    A) By avoiding any study on the day before the exam
    B) Through techniques such as deep breathing, visualization, or brief meditative practices
    C) By discussing their fears with other candidates just before the exam
    D) Focusing only on the hardest topics

36. What role does time management play in exam preparation?
    A) It ensures that less important topics are covered first
    B) It helps candidates to allocate sufficient time to study each topic thoroughly

C) It encourages candidates to study only at night

D) It decreases the overall effectiveness of study sessions

37. How should a candidate approach memorization for the exam?
    A) By memorizing facts in isolation
    B) Using mnemonic devices to improve recall
    C) Focusing solely on new information
    D) Avoiding repetitive review of material

38. What is a recommended action if a candidate does not know an answer during the exam?
    A) Guess immediately without skipping
    B) Mark the question and return to it after answering known questions
    C) Leave the question blank
    D) Spend additional time until the answer is remembered

39. How can physical well-being affect exam performance?
    A) It has no impact on mental state
    B) Adequate sleep, nutrition, and exercise can enhance cognitive function and endurance
    C) Only exercise on the day before the exam is beneficial
    D) Skipping meals before the exam increases focus

40. Why should candidates review the exam format and instructions carefully?
    A) It may contain tricks to confuse them
    B) Understanding the format can help manage time and approach during the exam
    C) The format changes frequently
    D) It is only necessary for first-time test takers

Chapter 5: Test Techniques and Tactics

41. Which strategy is most effective for ensuring a deep understanding of complex insurance topics?
    A) Regularly switching study topics to maintain interest
    B) Focusing on one topic until fully understood before moving to the next
    C) Reading through all topics once without taking notes
    D) Listening to relevant podcasts only

42. What is a beneficial practice the night before the exam?
    A) Starting a new topic to keep the mind active

B) Reviewing all notes and materials quickly for hours
C) Getting a full night's sleep
D) Planning an intensive study session with peers

43. How should a candidate utilize breaks during study sessions?
    A) To catch up on personal tasks
    B) To engage in light physical activity or relaxation to refresh the mind
    C) To discuss unrelated topics with peers
    D) To take extended naps

44. What is the purpose of taking timed practice exams?
    A) To understand the content deeply without focusing on time
    B) To stress the candidate out as much as possible
    C) To simulate actual exam conditions and improve time management
    D) To complete as many questions as possible without reviewing answers

45. What technique can help with retaining complex information?
    A) Avoiding the topic until the day before the exam
    B) Using mnemonic devices to create associations
    C) Focusing solely on rote memorization without understanding
    D) Reading information out loud once and hoping to remember

46. How can a candidate effectively deal with a difficult question during the exam?
    A) Spend as much time as needed, even if it impacts the ability to complete the exam
    B) Skip and return to it later after completing easier questions
    C) Immediately guess without fully reading the question
    D) Leave it blank and return only if there is extra time at the end

47. What should be the focus when selecting which practice exams to take?
    A) Only the easiest available to boost confidence
    B) Those that closely mimic the format and difficulty of the actual exam
    C) Unrelated practice exams for general knowledge
    D) Outdated exams for simplicity

48. Why is it important to study from multiple sources?
    A) To compare which source has the easiest content
    B) It confuses the candidate, making the actual exam easier by comparison
    C) To gain a broader perspective and more comprehensive understanding of complex topics
    D) To spend more time studying without focusing on exam relevance

49. What role does feedback play in preparing for the exam?
    A) It should be ignored to maintain confidence
    B) It is crucial for identifying weak areas and adjusting study habits
    C) It is only useful if it is positive
    D) Feedback should only be considered from non-experts for a challenge

50. How should a candidate approach the final week before the exam?
    A) Take a complete break from studying to clear the mind
    B) Intensely cram all materials every day until the exam
    C) Review key concepts and take care of physical and mental health
    D) Focus only on unfamiliar and new material

Mixed Multiple Choice Questions

51. What is the primary role of a broker in insurance?
    A) Underwriting insurance policies
B) Investing policy premiums
    C) Selling and servicing insurance policies on behalf of multiple insurers
    D) Assessing claims

52. Which type of policy feature is common in universal life insurance but not in term life insurance?
    A) Fixed premiums
    B) Investment component
    C) Fixed term
    D) Immediate payout

53. What does 'Risk Pooling' imply in the context of insurance?
    A) Distributing risk across various investment assets
    B) Combining various types of insurance into one package
    C) Sharing of risks over a large group to minimize the financial impact on any single member
    D) Centralizing the insurance funds for better management

54. What principle ensures that an insurance policy should not provide a benefit greater than the loss suffered by the insured?
   A) Insurable Interest
   B) Indemnity
   C) Utmost Good Faith
   D) Contribution

55. Which statement best describes term life insurance?
   A) It offers coverage for a lifetime with a savings component.
   B) It provides coverage for a specified period with no savings component.
   C) It allows the policyholder to invest in equity markets.
   D) It covers medical and surgical expenses.

56. What is typically covered by a critical illness rider in a life insurance policy?
   A) Funeral expenses
   B) Loss of income due to illness
   C) Immediate medical expenses
   D) Payments towards long-term treatments like chemotherapy

57. What is a deductible in an insurance policy?
   A) A premium discount for low-risk policyholders
   B) The amount a policyholder must pay out-of-pocket before the insurer pays a claim
   C) A refundable deposit paid at the start of the insurance term
   D) A bonus given for no claims

58. Which of these is a benefit of group life insurance?
   A) Higher premiums
   B) Customized policies for each individual
   C) Coverage without proof of insurability
   D) Investment options

59. What is typically NOT covered under standard health insurance policies?
   A) Emergency services
   B) Cosmetic surgery
   C) Prescription drugs
   D) Hospitalization

60. Which type of insurance policy combines high deductibles with a tax-advantaged savings option?
    A) Whole life insurance
    B) Term life insurance
    C) High-Deductible Health Plan (HDHP)
    D) Universal life insurance

61. Under what circumstance can the insured benefit from the 'Waiver of Premium' rider?
    A) If they decide to cancel the policy
    B) If they are diagnosed with a terminal illness
    C) If they are temporarily unemployed
    D) If they become disabled and unable to work

62. Which feature allows a variable life insurance policyholder to increase the potential investment gains?
    A) Fixed interest rate
    B) Investment options linked to the stock market
    C) Guaranteed minimum benefit
    D) Lifetime coverage

63. What is a common use of dividends in a participating life insurance policy?
    A) To increase the death benefit
    B) To decrease the premium payments
    C) Both A and B
    D) Neither A nor B

64. Which insurance principle protects against insurance fraud by ensuring policyholders do not profit from their loss?
    A) Proximate Cause
    B) Indemnity
    C) Contribution
    D) Subrogation

65. What is the primary function of reinsurance in the insurance industry?
    A) To increase the investment options available to primary insurers
    B) To allow insurers to underwrite more policies
    C) To decrease the overall risk by spreading it across another insurance company
    D) To provide loans to insurance companies

66. Which term describes the legal right of an insurer to pursue a third party that caused an insurance loss to the insured?
    A) Subrogation
    B) Indemnity
    C) Contribution
    D) Deductible

67. What does the underwriting process involve?
    A) Calculating the policy premium based on risk
    B) Determining the claims process
    C) Issuing dividends to policyholders
    D) Transferring policies between insurers

68. What does the 'Contestability Period' allow an insurer to do in life insurance?
    A) Change the premium rates based on market conditions
    B) Review the policy terms for any fraudulent information after a claim is made
    C) Convert the term life into whole life without medical underwriting
    D) Cancel the policy if the insured does not pay the premium

69. Which policy feature allows older individuals to receive health insurance regardless of their health status?
    A) Affordable Care Act mandates
    B) Guaranteed issue
    C) Group health insurance benefits
    D) No-fault insurance

70. What role does an actuary play in the insurance industry?
    A) Negotiating policy terms with clients
    B) Investing the premiums collected to fund claims
    C) Designing insurance products and calculating risks
    D) Processing claims and determining payouts

These questions and explanations will enrich readers' learning experience and enhance their readiness for the licensing exam by covering a broad range of essential topics in insurance.As discussed in the book, these questions are designed to review and reinforce the knowledge required for the Life and Health Insurance License Exam. Now that you have practiced with these questions move on to Section III, where you will find the solutions and explanations for each question. This section will help clarify any uncertainties and ensure you are well-prepared for your exam.

SECTION III

ANSWERS AND EXPLANATIONS

Chapter 1: Understanding the Fundamentals

1. **B) Provide financial security to dependents**

   • Life insurance is primarily designed to provide financial security for the policyholder's dependents in the event of their untimely death, ensuring that financial obligations can still be met.

2. **C) Major Medical Insurance**

   • Major medical insurance is best suited for covering significant medical expenses that occur due to illnesses or injuries, handling large claims such as hospital stays or emergency medical care, and not day-to-day expenses.

3. **D) Risk pooling**

   • Risk pooling is the fundamental insurance principle where risks are shared among a large group of people to minimize the financial impact on any single member caused by the loss of a few.

4. **B) The insurer and the insured have a mutual obligation to disclose all important facts.**

   • Utmost good faith, or uberrima fides, is a legal doctrine in insurance that requires all parties to act honestly and not mislead or withhold critical information from one another.

5. **B) Life insurance**

   • Life insurance is primarily designed to replace income in the event of the policyholder's death, ensuring financial stability for dependents.

6. **A) The term length**

   • The term length of a term life insurance policy directly influences the premium cost, as it determines the duration over which risk is covered.

7. **B) Lifetime coverage**

   • Whole Life Insurance is characterized by lifetime coverage, as opposed to term life insurance which only covers a specified period.

8. **B) Upon the policyholder's death**

   - The death benefit of a life insurance policy is typically paid out when the policyholder dies, providing financial support to beneficiaries.

9. **B) The policy owner must expect to benefit financially by the continued life of the insured.**

   - Insurable interest means the policy owner would suffer a financial loss from the death of the insured, which legitimizes the need for life insurance.

10. **C) Choosing not to engage in skydiving**

    - Risk avoidance involves taking steps to avoid activities that carry risk, such as choosing not to engage in dangerous sports like skydiving.

Chapter 2: Types of Insurance Policies

11. **B) Temporary versus permanent coverage**

    - Term Life Insurance provides temporary coverage with no cash value accumulation, while Whole Life Insurance offers permanent coverage with a cash value component.

12. **C) Universal Life Insurance**

    - Universal Life Insurance provides flexibility in premiums and the death benefit, allowing the policyholder to adjust the terms as their financial circumstances change.

13. **D) A mix of investments chosen by the policyholder**

    - Universal Life Insurance allows policyholders to select how their premiums are invested, offering a range of investment options to suit different risk tolerances.

14. **B) Investment options that can alter the value of the death benefit and cash value**

    - Variable Life Insurance includes investment options that can increase the policy's cash value and death benefit based on the performance of the underlying investments.

15. **B) High-net-worth individuals planning estate taxes**

    - Survivorship Life Insurance, or second-to-die insurance, covers two people and pays out upon the death of the second, often used for estate planning.

16. **D) Rider**

- A rider is an additional provision added to an insurance policy that provides benefits not included in the main policy, such as covering a spouse or child.

17. **B) Employer benefit packages**

- Group Life Insurance is typically offered through employer benefit packages, providing coverage to employees under a single master policy.

18. **B) Convert the term policy into a whole or universal life policy without a medical exam**

- Convertible Term Life Insurance allows the policyholder to convert their term life policy into a permanent one without undergoing a new medical exam, providing continuous coverage.

19. **B) Whole Life Insurance**

- Whole Life Insurance policies often include an automatic premium loan feature, which allows unpaid premiums to be covered by a loan against the policy's cash value.

20. **C) Both A and B**

- In a Whole Life policy, the cash value accumulates on a tax-deferred basis and is accessible through withdrawals and policy loans, providing financial flexibility to the policyholder.

Chapter 3: Insurance Regulations

21. **B) Regulating and overseeing insurance companies within the state**

- State insurance departments are primarily responsible for regulating and overseeing the activities of insurance companies within their jurisdictions, ensuring compliance with state laws and regulations.

22. **B) National Association of Insurance Commissioners, an organization that helps set standards and regulations**

- The NAIC (National Association of Insurance Commissioners) plays a key role in standardizing regulatory practices across states to ensure a consistent approach to insurance regulation.

23. **B) They may vary significantly from state to state, affecting how insurance is practiced locally**

   - State-specific regulations can differ widely, impacting how insurance policies are written, sold, and managed in different states.

   -

24. **B) To ensure compliance with insurance regulations through reviews of practices and procedures**

   - Market conduct examinations are conducted to ensure that insurance companies are complying with regulatory standards and are not engaging in practices that could harm consumers.

25. **B) It protects consumers from unfair practices and ensures fair treatment**

   - Consumer protection is crucial in the insurance industry to safeguard the rights of policyholders and ensure they are treated fairly by insurers.

26. **C) Deceptive, misleading, or fraudulent conduct by those in the insurance industry**

   - Unfair trade practices in insurance involve any actions by insurers or agents that deceive, mislead, or defraud customers.

27. **B) Misuse of insurance funds and deceptive practices**

   - Fraud and abuse regulation in the insurance industry aims to prevent the misuse of funds and stop practices that deceive or defraud policyholders.

28. **B) By ensuring that insurance professionals are qualified and knowledgeable**

   - Licensing requirements ensure that individuals selling insurance or advising on insurance matters are adequately qualified to provide accurate and reliable information to consumers.

29. **B) They help maintain high professional standards and up-to-date knowledge**

- Continuing education requirements ensure that insurance professionals continue to update their knowledge and maintain high professional standards throughout their careers.

30. **C) Through state insurance department investigations and resolutions**

- Complaints against insurance companies are typically handled through investigations and resolutions carried out by state insurance departments, ensuring that grievances are addressed fairly.

Chapter 4: Preparing for the Exam

31. **C) Engaging with the material through teaching or group discussions**

- Engaging deeply with the material, such as through teaching or discussing with peers, helps solidify understanding and enhance retention, making it an effective study technique.

32. **C) Quickly answer easy questions to allow more time for difficult ones**

- Managing time effectively during the exam by quickly answering easier questions ensures that there is sufficient time left to tackle more challenging questions.

33. **C) Relying on practice exams as the sole form of study**

- While practice exams are an essential part of exam preparation, relying solely on them without engaging with other forms of study materials or techniques is a common mistake.

34. **B) To minimize anxiety and establish a mental readiness for the exam**

- Developing a routine for exam day helps minimize anxiety and puts you in the right mental state to tackle the exam effectively.

35. **B) Through techniques such as deep breathing, visualization, or brief meditative practices**

   - Techniques like deep breathing, visualization, and meditation are effective in mitigating test anxiety, helping maintain calm and focus during the exam.

36. **B) It helps candidates to allocate sufficient time to study each topic thoroughly**

   - Effective time management in exam preparation ensures sufficient time for each topic, allowing for a thorough understanding and review.

37. **B) Using mnemonic devices to improve recall**

   - Mnemonic devices are useful for improving recall, making them a recommended method for memorizing complex or voluminous information for the exam.

38. **B) Mark the question and return to it after answering known questions**

   - If unsure about an answer, it's best to mark the question and return to it after addressing known questions, maximizing scoring potential.

39. **B) Adequate sleep, nutrition, and exercise can enhance cognitive function and endurance**

   - Maintaining good physical health, including getting enough sleep, proper nutrition, and regular exercise, can significantly boost cognitive function and endurance, enhancing exam performance.

40. **B) Understanding the format can help manage time and approach during the exam**

   - Familiarizing oneself with the exam format and instructions helps in better time management and strategic approach during the exam, avoiding confusion and maximizing efficiency.

41. B) Focusing on one topic until fully understood before moving to the next

- Deeply understanding each topic before moving to the next ensures a comprehensive grasp of the material, which is critical for effective exam preparation.

42. C) Getting a full night's sleep

- Ensuring a full night's sleep before the exam day helps maintain alertness and cognitive clarity, which are crucial for optimal performance.

43. B) To engage in light physical activity or relaxation to refresh the mind

- Taking breaks to engage in light physical activity or relaxation techniques during study sessions can help refresh the mind, improve focus, and enhance retention.

44. C) To simulate actual exam conditions and improve time management

- Taking timed practice exams helps simulate real exam conditions, which is essential for improving time management skills and getting accustomed to the pressure of the actual exam.

45. B) Using mnemonic devices to create associations

- Employing mnemonic devices to create memorable associations makes it easier to recall complex information during the exam.

46. B) Skip and return to it later after completing easier questions

- If a question is too difficult, it's efficient to skip it and return later, ensuring that easier questions are completed first to secure all possible points.

47. B) Those that closely mimic the format and difficulty of the actual exam

- Selecting practice exams that closely reflect the actual exam format and difficulty level is crucial for realistic practice and effective preparation.

48. C) To gain a broader perspective and more comprehensive understanding of complex topics

- Studying from multiple sources helps expand one's perspective and fosters a more comprehensive understanding of the material, essential for tackling diverse exam questions.

49. B) It is crucial for identifying weak areas and adjusting study habits

- Feedback plays a vital role in identifying areas of weakness and allows for adjustments in study habits, ensuring more focused and effective preparation.

50. C) Review key concepts and take care of physical and mental health

- In the final week before the exam, reviewing key concepts and maintaining good physical and mental health is important, preparing for peak performance on exam day.

Mixed Multiple Choice Answers

51. C) Selling and servicing insurance policies on behalf of multiple insurers

A broker represents the client and deals with several insurers, unlike agents who represent one insurance company.

52. B) Investment component

Universal life insurance includes an investment component that accumulates cash value, unlike term life which does not.

53. C) Sharing of risks over a large group to minimize the financial impact on any single member

Risk pooling is a fundamental insurance principle where the risks are shared among a large group to lower the financial impact on any individual within the group.

54. B) Indemnity

The principle of indemnity ensures that an insurance policy compensates for the loss without allowing the insured to profit from the claim.

55. B) It provides coverage for a specified period with no savings component.

Term life insurance is characterized by its provision of coverage for a set term without an investment or savings component.

56. D) Payments towards long-term treatments like chemotherapy

Critical illness riders typically cover severe health conditions by providing a lump sum to assist with the costs of long-term treatments.

57. B) The amount a policyholder must pay out-of-pocket before the insurer pays a claim

A deductible is a cost-sharing feature that requires the policyholder to pay a certain amount out-of-pocket before insurance coverage kicks in.

58. C) Coverage without proof of insurability

Group life insurance allows individuals to obtain insurance without individual proof of insurability, making it easier for all group members to be covered.

59. B) Cosmetic surgery

Standard health insurance policies typically do not cover cosmetic surgery as it is considered non-essential and elective.

60. C) High-Deductible Health Plan (HDHP)

HDHPs are health insurance plans with higher deductibles than typical health plans, often combined with a health savings account to provide tax benefits.

61. D) If they become disabled and unable to work

The waiver of premium rider exempts the insured from paying the policy premiums if they become disabled and are unable to work.

62. B) Investment options linked to the stock market

Variable life insurance policies allow policyholders to invest the cash value in various securities, offering potential for higher returns based on market performance.

63. C) Both A and B

Dividends from a participating life insurance policy can be used either to purchase additional insurance or to reduce future premiums, thereby enhancing the policy's value or affordability.

64. B) Indemnity

The principle of indemnity is designed to prevent policyholders from profiting from their insurance coverage, ensuring they only receive compensation equivalent to the loss suffered.

65. C) To decrease the overall risk by spreading it across another insurance company

Reinsurance allows primary insurers to share the risks associated with their insured policies with other insurers, mitigating potential large losses.

66. A) Subrogation

Subrogation allows an insurer to step into the shoes of the insured, to seek recovery or enforce the rights of the insured against a third party responsible for the insurance loss.

67. A) Calculating the policy premium based on risk

The underwriting process involves evaluating the risk associated with an applicant to determine the premium rates and coverage terms.

68. B) Review the policy terms for any fraudulent information after a claim is made

The contestability period is a time frame during which an insurer can review and contest a claim and the policy terms to check for any misrepresentation or fraud at the policy inception.

69. B) Guaranteed issue

Guaranteed issue is a feature mandated by the Affordable Care Act, ensuring that older individuals and those with pre-existing conditions can obtain health insurance without being denied coverage based on their health status.

70. C) Designing insurance products and calculating risks

Actuaries are professionals who specialize in calculating risks and designing insurance products to ensure the financial stability and pricing adequacy of insurance offerings.

These solutions and explanations help clarify each concept and ensure you are well-prepared for the Life and Health Insurance License Exam. Good luck with your studying and future exam!

CONCLUSION AND BONUS

As we end this in-depth guide to preparing for the Life and Health Insurance Licence exam, it's essential to take a step back and appreciate the breadth of knowledge you've acquired and the depth of the path you've chosen in the insurance industry. Critical to the financial well-being of individuals and businesses alike, this field relies on dedicated professionals like you who are equipped with extensive knowledge and driven by a commitment to serve and protect.

Entering the insurance world is more than a career choice - it is a commitment to continuous learning and ethical practice. Every concept you master, from policy types to regulatory nuances, enriches your ability to secure the future of others. Remember, your role goes beyond transactions; you are a provider of stability in times of uncertainty.

The ever-evolving landscape of insurance, shaped by legislative, technological and economic changes, requires an ongoing commitment to education. The need to stay current is as much about maintaining competence as it is about providing the best possible service to those who rely on your expertise. Your adaptability and continuous growth will mark your success in the field.

Approaching the exam is a daunting challenge requiring a strategic and disciplined mindset. The strategies discussed here are designed to give you the tools to face this challenge confidently. Overcoming test anxiety, managing your study time effectively and mastering the exam format are hurdles you will be well prepared to overcome. Remember, your success on exam day is a strong indicator of your readiness to face the real challenges of your career.

Ethics and professionalism are the cornerstones of your insurance practice. They ensure that the trust your customers place in you is never misplaced. As you build your career, let integrity be your unwavering guide, and let every decision you make reinforce the trust that defines your professional relationships. Networking and engagement with the wider insurance community are invaluable to professional development. These connections provide a wealth of resources, advice and support, enhancing your understanding and skills within the industry. They also provide platforms for discussing emerging trends and common challenges, enriching your professional journey with diverse perspectives and new opportunities.

As you prepare for the exam, recognize the effort and dedication that has brought you to this point. Your preparation is significant, but it's only the beginning of what promises to be a rewarding career. The opportunities to make a difference to people's lives through your work are vast and meaningful. After the exam, your path will continue to unfold with endless possibilities for growth and impact. Whether you're crafting policies to protect families or guiding businesses through risk management, the knowledge you take with you will serve as your compass. Continue to seek out new learning opportunities and expand your professional network.

Let this guide serve as a companion to your exam preparation and as a fundamental blueprint for a fulfilling career in insurance. You are stepping into a role characterized by service, expertise, and integrity. Seize this opportunity to make a meaningful difference in the lives of others. We wish you the best of luck in your exam and the many years of your successful career. Remember, with every customer interaction, you are reaffirming the vital role of insurance in building a secure and hopeful future for all. Your journey is just beginning, and the possibilities are as limitless as your commitment.

As we conclude this guide, we hope it has provided you with a comprehensive framework for your exam preparation and future career in the insurance industry. We're committed to ensuring that the information presented here is accurate and useful. If you have any suggestions or observations or would like to share feedback that could enhance the clarity or depth of the material, please feel free to reach out. Your input is invaluable and will help improve the guidance provided to future readers as they embark on this important professional journey.

Blueprint Institute

Download here the bonus! Scar the QR code or go to the link below to download more than 600 state-specific questions and printable flashcards

https://bit.ly/blueprintinstitutebonuslifeandhealth

Made in the USA
Las Vegas, NV
30 June 2024

91684667R00059